TRUMP
ON THE COUCH

TRUMP

ON THE COUCH

INSIDE THE MIND
OF THE PRESIDENT

JUSTIN A. FRANK, MD

AVERY

AN IMPRINT OF PENGUIN RANDOM HOUSE

AVERY

an imprint of Penguin Random House LLC
375 Hudson Street
New York, New York 10014

The author gratefully acknowledges permission to quote from the following:

"Old Man Trump," words and music by Woody Guthrie and Ryan Harvey.
Copyright © 2016 Woody Guthrie Publications Inc. and Ryan Harvey Music.
All Rights for Woody Guthrie Publications Inc. Administered by BMG Rights
Management (US) LLC. All Rights Reserved. Used by Permission. *Reprinted
by Permission of Hal Leonard LLC.*

"Mock Confessional," by Lawrence Ferlinghetti, from *These Are My Rivers,*
copyright © 1973 by Lawrence Ferlinghetti. Reprinted by permission of New
Directions Publishing Corp.

Most Avery books are available at special quantity discounts for bulk purchase for
sales promotions, premiums, fund-raising, and educational needs. Special books or
book excerpts also can be created to fit specific needs. For details, write
SpecialMarkets@penguinrandomhouse.com.

ISBN 9780735220324

Printed in the United States of America
1   3   5   7   9   10   8   6   4   2

Book design by Amy Hill

To Karen and Steve Scheinman,
dearly loved lifelong friends

Whoever is careless with the truth in small matters
cannot be trusted with important matters.

—ALBERT EINSTEIN

CONTENTS

INTRODUCTION

I have a feeling I'm falling
On rare occasions
But most of the time I have my feet on the ground
I can't help it if the ground itself is falling.

—Lawrence Ferlinghetti

There is something really raw about the ground
shaking. As humans, we think we can rely on
solid ground. If that shakes, too, it shakes you to
the bones.

—Francis Cristobal, resident of Hilo, Hawaii, 2018

Trump on the Couch is a book I never expected to write. Midway through George W. Bush's first presidential term, my concerns about Bush's mental health led me to undertake an in-depth exploration of his psyche, using the discipline of applied psychoanalysis—the practice of applying psychoanalytic principles to the consideration of the motivations and limitations of historical figures, which Sigmund

Freud pioneered when he was developing his theories of self and psychoanalysis. In 2004, I published my findings in *Bush on the Couch*, which struck a chord with readers and demonstrated that applied psychoanalysis can shed unique and invaluable light on who our current leaders are—and how they got that way.

My second book reprised the applied psychoanalytic approach to explore the psyche of a much different, if still enigmatic, individual, drawing in part upon his extensive writings to trace his psychological development. In *Obama on the Couch* I described our forty-fourth president as suffering from "Obsessive Bipartisan Disorder," a characterological need to avoid partisan positioning that was rooted in his biography as the son of a broken, mixed-race marriage; as we have learned more about the motivations behind Obama's remaining silent about the Russian manipulation of the 2016 election, it has become painfully clear that his Obsessive Bipartisan Disorder did indeed set the stage for Trump's victory and attempts to eradicate Obama's record. Published in 2011 in the early years of the Tea Party, *Obama on the Couch* also explored the psychological underpinnings of some of the positions embraced by the Republican opposition, as well as the psychological blind spots that enabled Obama's and the Democrats' failure to appreciate fully the strength of that opposition. I concluded with my concern that these unexamined pockets of denial could pave the way for a successor who poses even graver risks to the nation and the world than did his predecessor.

Donald Trump is in part a logical product of those blind spots. We are faced with a president whose mental health is widely and openly questioned, and an awakening on the Left to the depth of the hostility with which the Right views them. Much has been written about Trump's psyche during the 2016 campaign and the first year of his presidency, but very little was actually grounded in psychoanalytic theory. That said, *Trump on the Couch* is likely not the first in-depth attempt to try to define Trump's personality and character through the discipline of applied psychoanalysis. However, I can't say I've read the treatises that I suspect have preceded my own, because I don't speak Russian.

The discipline of applied psychoanalysis has long been used by the CIA and other intelligence agencies to study foreign leaders and politicians, and I have no doubt that the Russian effort to interfere on Trump's behalf in the 2016 election was preceded by an extensive assessment of his psyche. Russian intelligence has access to the same psychoanalytic theory as American intelligence agencies (and psychoanalysts); assuming the Russians ground that theory into a lens through which to carefully review Trump's known biography, what they would have seen was a person who was uniquely positioned to be coopted—knowingly or unknowingly, or both—by an authoritative Putin regime looking to manipulate America's voters and destabilize its democracy at home and influence abroad.

My analytic approach is informed by the Freudian tradition as well as the work of psychoanalytical theorist Melanie Klein, who expanded on Freud's discoveries and focused in particular on the mental attitudes that the individual demonstrates toward aggression and destructiveness. As Trump has quickly established himself as the most aggressive, destructive president in memory, the Kleinian approach is particularly apt for understanding him. Klein posits that the individual's struggle to manage his own innate destructiveness begins in early childhood, and we will use that insight as a tool for understanding a broad range of Trump's behaviors.

As a Kleinian, my approach to analyzing the last two presidents' psyches has relied heavily on previously published biographical information about their childhoods and their families. The historical record on Trump's family and early years is considerably thinner by comparison, but remarkably revealing. We will work with what we've got. Fortunately, Donald Trump's own published record—from books he has authored over the years to his more recent, incomparable Twitter output—provides an unprecedented amount of material that depicts how these unconscious patterns developed in childhood still influence his words and deeds in adulthood.

This book is divided into two parts. Part one will look at Trump's family history and early years to identify the sources of the dynamics that are most essential to understanding Trump's psychology. In part two, we'll look at a range of defenses and disorders that he demonstrates as an adult, with an eye toward identifying their psychoanalytic underpinnings as a means toward understanding their influence as well as his defenses against their impact. Finally, a glossary will revisit some of the terms that have been central to our discussion.

Psychoanalysis, as practiced in the consulting room, is not a linear process. We start where the patient is at the moment and eventually spiral around and around from past to present, from dreams to reality, from wishes to actions—and then back again. Sometimes the first dream a patient describes can contain all the issues of a complete analysis, and becomes something to which we return time and again.

This means that we will often return to familiar material from Trump's life, but with different perspectives that depend on his particular behavior at the time. Reexamining fundamental conflicts, called "working through" in the consulting room, is a way of showing how underlying core character traits or meanings are recognizable in different circumstances. Readers may often find themselves "working through" by recognizing the essential Trump in various settings. We see repetition of Trump's childhood patterns, anxieties, and the behaviors he has employed to address (or avoid) them.

Listening to the patient's associations, thoughts, and feelings results in the analyst having to choose a point on which to comment—what's called a "selected emotional fact," i.e., something the analyst selects because of its affective content, or the way it seems to repeat, or its proximity to the patient's anxieties. A patient's thought patterns are sometimes obviously linked, but sometimes harder to follow because they are connected only unconsciously—sort of like when math teachers ask students to "show" their work and not just supply the answers.

Sometimes in the consulting room, the patient cannot show his or her work because it takes place outside conscious awareness. Trump presents a particular problem, however, because his fundamental behavior is often segmented and disconnected even unconsciously from what he has said or done previously. This makes it harder to follow him than to follow other public figures—though one can see repeated actions that give us vivid clues to his character.

This book is in part aimed to help readers see that we know more about Trump and other public figures than we may realize—if we pay attention. Someone like fired FBI director James Comey is a good example of a sensitive person who, while not explicitly trained in psychoanalysis, understands Trump profoundly. As he said to David Remnick in a *New Yorker* interview, "I think he has an emptiness inside of him, and a hunger for affirmation, that I've never seen in an adult."

THERE'S NO QUESTION THAT Trump is mentally unfit in ways that make him psychologically unsuited for the presidency; this is in itself a truly alarming turn of events, and I would write the entire book in all caps if I thought that would better convey the sense of urgency with which it is written and should be read. Any number of troubling mental-illness diagnoses and character evaluations can be (and have been) accurately applied to Trump; both can vary from analyst to analyst, however, without necessarily sacrificing any of the accuracy. More to the point, the true value of a diagnosis is to determine an appropriate course of treatment—and there is no indication that any sort of treatment is a viable option.

Trump on the Couch, then, seeks not simply to make the case that Trump is not well, but rather to show how he is unwell in ways that would have been of particular interest to the applied psychoanalysts whose investigation likely preceded our own— the Russians (and perhaps even their American allies or counterparts) who in the long tradition of intelligence-gathering examined Trump's psyche and found an opportunity for exploitation. Trump's presidency caps a lifetime of dysfunction and disorder that is not likely to be healed while he is in office, just as Trump's ascendency among voters gives expression to long-standing trends in the American electorate's psyche that are not going to be easily addressed. However, if we can identify certain aspects of those disorders and trends that may have contributed to Trump and his voters fusing into a shared belief system, then we have a better chance of fostering the kind of honest cultural discussion that will be necessary in order to contain and begin to repair the damage that has already been done.

UNDERSTANDING TRUMP CALLS FOR a consideration of his psychodynamics almost certainly more rigorous than he has ever embarked upon on his own. Trump dismissed psychotherapy as "a crutch" in his 2004 *Playboy* interview; years later, talking to biographer Michael D'Antonio, he described in greater detail a general aversion to introspection beyond the therapeutic setting. "I don't like to analyze myself because I might not like what I see," he told D'Antonio. "I don't like to analyze myself. I don't like to think too much about the past."

Even armed with a detailed family history, we can't capture Trump in action with only the tools of applied psychoanalysis. Like some of the most disturbed patients I've worked with, Trump is so erratic—constantly changing the topic, elevating the stakes, and raising the volume—that one doesn't know what to expect from him next. It's hard to imagine him in treatment; even as the subject of an applied psychoanalytical investigation, he behaves like a patient who is simultaneously banging at the consulting room window, rattling at its door, ringing the phone and texting—or tweeting—his demands for attention.

Trump presents so many troubling affects that it is hard to remember them all. In the final weeks of the first year of Trump's presidency, Michael Wolff and David Cay Johnston published accounts of the Trump White House that present a president with a startling number of disturbing characteristics. Any one of these demonstrable and suspected traits would raise calls for a psychoanalytic investigation in a layperson. In a president, in the aggregate, they are truly cause for alarm.

The list of worrisome evident and alleged attributes that emerge in these and other portraits is long. Narcissist. Liar. Racist. Sexist. Adulterer. Baby. Hypocrite. Chiseler. Tax cheat. Outlaw. Psychopath. Paranoid. Fraud. Ignorant. Vengeful. Delusional. Arrogant. Greedy. Contemptuous. Unsympathetic. Learning disabled. Cruel. Obstructer of justice. Threat to the Constitution. Traitor.

The list is so long that it can be overwhelming—it's a challenge to remember the beginning by the time you make it to the end. There are times when I wish someone would help us remember all the troubling aspects of Trump's character and behavior, past and present, in a way that would encourage recognition of the totality of his pathology, rather than its component parts, which individually cause alarm before being temporarily forgotten when the next emergency presents itself.

As an applied psychoanalyst, my task is not only to appreciate the full list but also to ignore the big picture and focus on a single pathology at a time. Practitioners of applied psychoanalysis approach their subject as both theoretician and clinician. The theoretician endeavors to piece things together, to figure things out, while the clinician tries to approach each session capable of being surprised, as if his mind were a blank slate. The analysis in the following pages aspires to accomplish both goals—reviewing Trump's record with a clinician's eye, preparing to be surprised by the unexpected observation, and assembling those findings into a more comprehensive portrait.

The image of hypothetical patient Trump rattling the

consulting room door and banging on the window reminds us that President Trump doesn't want us to see the entire list at once. Not only that, but patients I've treated who are reminiscent of Trump cannot tolerate being inside the consulting room either; they leave my office whenever they feel unable to think their way through an anxiety-provoking interpretation—much the way Trump leaves press briefings when the questions get too close.

Trump is also invested in our being surprised by his distractions, aimed at preventing us from connecting the dots to see patterns that might yield a genuinely illuminating portrait. He is counting on our inability to construct a full picture from his various traits and questionable activities, to forget the disturbing revelations of the past, to operate without the kind of astute and holistic perspective that would keep all his various pathologies front of mind to help us process and remember. And it would be impossible to run after him if he walked out, unless I were working on a closed psychiatric ward.

In his indispensable *It's Even Worse Than You Think*, David Cay Johnston uses the term "con artist" to describe Trump freely and frequently enough to earn it a place on the list above. It won't be found in the pages that follow, but it's worth noting that the con artist operates with the confidence that most of his observers will not make the mental connections that would help them see the patterns he doesn't want them to see. Donald Trump conducts himself with an almost intuitive understanding of the limits of typical human perception, which are confirmed by the news media's apparent inability to remember his behaviors and disorders—even from a few weeks earlier. Now it's easier with video and sound recordings, but even those require hours to review.

This book is an attempt to help readers see connections and patterns in Trump's pathology that may have previously escaped notice. It invites readers to contemplate both the specifics of the way Trump's mind operates and the bigger picture that emerges. The stakes for our nation could not be higher.

PART ONE

ORIGINS

Chapter One

MOTHER

A lad out of control brings disgrace to his mother.

⁓*Proverbs 29:15*

I t all begins with the mother.

My approach to applied psychoanalysis always starts with the dynamic between infant and mother. Melanie Klein, an Austrian British pioneer in the psychoanalysis of children— from the generation after Freud—developed her revolutionary theories by observing young children's actual interactions with mothers and primary caregivers, and expanded them into a framework that can help the applied psychoanalyst draw upon the historical record to illuminate the echoes of these early relationships. In Klein's construct, the interactions between the infant and his mother play a determinative role in shaping essential elements of the individual's relationships with the self, with others, and with the outside world that develop over a lifetime and profoundly influence the adult's psychological outlook and health.

Not surprisingly, Kleinian analysis joins the long list of precedents and protocols for which Donald Trump presents a unique challenge, if not an outright disruption. Less has been written about the details of Donald Trump's early biography in general, and about his mother in particular, than has been written about any US president in recent memory. Perhaps the thinness of the historical record contributes to so many Trump observers asking how an individual could develop such a temperament, let alone get elected president. The dearth of biographical detail lends added resonance to the questions that occupied so many of us in 2017, such as: What happened? How did we get here? How did *he* get here?

We can hope that future historians and biographers will more closely examine Trump's life story to gain further insight into the events of his formative years that contributed to the development of a character so profoundly lacking in the attributes appropriate for the office he was so tenaciously compelled to pursue. As a Kleinian, I'm particularly hopeful that attention will be paid to Trump's relationship with his mother, which I am predisposed to thinking will offer valuable insight into his psychological development.

The Kleinian approach can help identify early childhood dynamics, which can influence the adult's attitudes toward the capacity to feel empathy for others, the ability to mourn, and the capacity to take responsibility for one's own behavior—especially acknowledging one's own destructive or cruel behavior, without having to blame others. Only by facing one's own destructive fantasies and actions can one be able genuinely to love others. Otherwise it always feels phony or put-on. This failure helps us see Trump's comfort with conning others, with exaggerating what he can do in a seemingly real way while remaining deceptive.

It is the self-deception for which he might ultimately pay a price, but in the interval, many Americans are already paying. One criterion for my psychiatric residency, something implicitly understood and openly discussed with fellow residents, was that successful psychiatric residents must be aware of their own sadism. Trump's grandiosity and need for attention are lifelong attempts to compensate for and deny the pain of self-recognition. It's unlikely by now for him to want to discover the intrapsychic processes at play that have brought him to where he is today.

Nevertheless, despite what could almost be seen as a deliberate or conscious attempt on Trump's part to do otherwise, the historical record does yield enough information about his mother and their relationship to shed some valuable light on the potential origins of what we now recognize as Trump's character. If Donald Trump walked into my office as a patient, once I got beyond the obvious first question (about which more later), I would want to know about his early childhood. Without asking him directly, I would listen closely to any discussion of his early years for clues about his capacity to form long-term relationships, his capacity to tolerate disappointments and frustration, and also what qualities he has that he is most proud of. In the absence of that opportunity, however, we can return to what he and others have said and written about his mother, Mary Trump, to create a distinct picture of how her conduct as a mother could have contributed to Trump's tendencies to lie, to brag, to bully others, and to evade taking responsibility for those and other behaviors.

The portrait of Mary Trump that can be drawn from available resources is by no means comprehensive, and lacks the detail of previous portraits of Stanley Ann Dunham or Barbara Bush. But what we do know about her is consistent enough to form a distinct image of Mary Trump as a person and as a mother—and of Donald Trump. And even if the portrait of Mary Trump that emerges is less detailed than the more familiar portrait of Donald's father, Fred Trump—who Donald cites as the bigger influence in his life—the assembled pieces fit together to delineate a mother-son dynamic that offers a lot to any consideration of what made him the man he is today.

First let's consider what we do know about Mary Trump, whose relatively low profile in Trump's published universe inspired *Politico*'s Michael Kruse to describe her as "a ghost in [Trump's] voluminous public record, a cardboard cutout of a character" in his November 2017 article "The Mystery of Mary Trump," which set out to add some much-needed detail to the known portrait of the president's mother, and to highlight the general rarity and vagueness of Donald's references to her.

As the public was reminded during Trump's early 2017 crackdown on immigration policies, Mary Anne MacLeod, an eighteen-year-old fleeing rural poverty, and the youngest of ten children with minimal prospects in her homeland, arrived in New York City from Scotland in 1930. After six years of working as a domestic and nanny, including a period for a wealthy Long Island family, she married Fred Trump, an already up-and-coming real estate developer. They started having children in 1937—Maryanne, the eldest, followed by Fred Jr. in 1938, Elizabeth in 1942, and Donald in 1946. By the time she had her fifth and final child, Robert, in 1948, Fred had moved his family into the biggest house on the biggest lot in the Queens neighborhood of Jamaica Estates, and Mary had hired her own Scottish maid. Robert's birth was difficult, followed by near-fatal hemorrhaging and a series of subsequent life-threatening infections and surgeries, which required several years of recovery and left Mary in fragile health thereafter. Still, Mary took to the life of being a prosperous real estate tycoon's wife, managing a house with servants, busying herself with volunteer work, and famously riding around Queens in a rose-colored Rolls-Royce with vanity plates, collecting the change from her husband's buildings' laundry machines. She stood by her wealthy husband—reportedly a notorious philanderer—until his death in 1999, following him to the grave a year later.

Beyond the known facts of her life, Donald Trump has had remarkably little to say about his mother. It's certainly well known that she wasn't as big an influence in his life as his father; in *Politico*, Kruse quotes a former staffer as saying that his mother's likeness was "noticeably absent" from his Trump

Tower office, where the only photograph on his desk was that of his father—which for Trump's first few months in the Oval Office was the only photo behind his desk, until he later added his mother's portrait. The absence is consistent with how a former business associate and close friend contrasts the two relationships to Kruse, saying that Trump "was in awe of his father . . . and very detached from his mother"—so much so, Kruse points out, that he misspelled her maiden name in his 2009 book, *Think Like a Champion*.

The most cogent explanation for the absence of Mary Trump from her son's memory and frame of mind is that it is reflective of her absence from his presence growing up. In Kruse's account, which ranks as the most detailed look into his mother's role in Donald's life, Mary Trump simply wasn't very present in Donald's childhood. Kruse reports that Trump's childhood friends attest to her absence: Mark Golding, described as "an early pal," reports that while Trump's father "would be around and watch him play," his mother "didn't interact in that way." Brother Fred's friend Lou Droesch says that the neighborhood kids "rarely saw Mrs. Trump," although they "did see a lot of the housekeeper"—especially noteworthy because of Mary's line of work before marrying Fred Trump, perhaps suggesting that she saw the work of mothering as something to be delegated to the help. It is also possible that as the tenth child, Mary may have been mothered more by her older siblings than by her own mother.

When neighborhood kids would come over to play, Mary

Trump usually would not make an appearance, Kruse reports, only Fred, who "would come down to say hello after work. 'He was more willing to play with us, if you will, than his mom,' Golding says." Another childhood friend tells Kruse that sometimes "the maid would appear with a platter of finger sandwiches with the crusts cut off. 'Like you'd serve at a cocktail party,' says Lou Droesch, who also spent time at the Trump house as a boy." Playmates who were invited to stay for dinner report, "The meal was formal in feel if simple in cuisine." When both parents were present, only one did most of the talking. "'Fred was fairly strict and wanted to know how everybody's days went,'" another friend, Paul Onish, told Kruse. "And Trump's mother? 'I don't remember Mary talking that much.'"

Donald and his siblings appeared to accept their mother's remoteness. "They spoke well of their mom, or never had a harsh word," Kruse reports Droesch told him, "but she just did not interact with the kids when their friends were around." Another childhood friend points out that Trump did talk about his father, especially his telling him to be "a king" and "a killer," but adds that Donald "didn't tell [him] what his mother's advice was. He didn't say anything about her. Not a word."

One theory about Donald's mother's scant presence in her children's lives traces her absence back to her poor health. It's certainly a plausible scenario that Mary would retreat to a life out of sight of her children's playmates if her health was just too fragile to allow otherwise. But Kruse describes her life after her recovery as a "busy routine," including "her volunteering, her ladies' luncheons," and her coin-collecting trips to her husband's properties, suggesting that a lack of stamina wasn't the reason behind her low family profile.

Biographer Gwenda Blair reports a remarkable story that would stand out even if it weren't so relatively rare in its offering particulars of Trump family life. For her family biography *The Trumps*, Blair spoke to Donald's eldest sister, Maryanne Trump Barry, who told Blair that during her mother's illness her father "came home and told me she wasn't expected to live . . . but I should go to school and he'd call me if anything changed. That's right—go to school as usual!" The command to his daughter speaks volumes about Fred's lack of compassion, of course, but also suggests that Mary's absence from the family must have been already established before she was almost entirely and permanently removed from it. It also speaks to Fred's powerful work ethic, which eclipsed all else in family life. Such circumstances leave no room for the children to express anxiety or concern—especially since they could use their worries as excuses to stay home from school. Fred was always suspicious of potential slackers. Maryanne just rolled her eyes, seemingly dismissive of her father's strict demands.

When a mother is as disengaged as the Mary Trump portrayed in these anecdotes, the absence can reverberate throughout her children's lifetimes. As readers familiar with the Kleinian approach of my previous books may recall, the adverse impact of the lack of a nurturing maternal presence can last a lifetime.

The relationship between mother and infant can provide an early blueprint for the model of the child's inner world that influences all his subsequent relationships. The mother serves as the first object of the infant's focus, and when he is being contentedly fed by an attentive mother, he experiences her as a loving extension of himself. The baby's positive experiences at the breast—which we use as a metaphor for the mother, regardless of how the baby is fed—forges his capacity to connect with a source of loving nourishment, the vital core of enduring self-esteem. The mother's loving smiles and warmth provide connection and emotional nourishment. But negative experiences can have a lasting impact as well, and a deprived or uncomfortable baby could visualize the breast as the source of his discomfort, and experience a distracted or disengaged mother as the source of frustration.

Lacking the ability to perceive that he derives both contentment and frustration from the same breast, the baby develops two primitive but distinct relationships with two different ideas of mother—one with the good breast/good mother, with whom he has a positive relationship that helps him manage his frustration, the other with the bad breast/bad mother, who is experienced as the source of the frustration that she is not helping him manage. The baby sees his own essential goodness in the good mother, and projects the unmanageable negative feelings onto the bad mother.

This primitive perspective is of only temporary usefulness, however, and the baby runs the risk of forever distorting his lifelong perceptions of the universe if he doesn't move beyond this simplistic approach to understanding his world. The mother plays a central role in this next stage of development, helping her baby transform his discomfort and anxiety into more manageable feelings. By sensing the baby's emotions and reacting accordingly, the mother processes the baby's experience and returns the feelings to the child in a form he can more easily tolerate. This leads the baby to develop his own sense of his emotions, empowering him to internalize the maternal function and transforming the bad feelings on his own, while remaining connected to his mother.

In this next stage of healthy development, the infant recognizes he has not two mothers but one, who is able both to comfort and disappoint him; this leads to the understanding that he can love and hate the same person, from which stems his essential capacity to experience ambivalence, as well as to internalize and recognize that the destructiveness he had previously projected comes from within. The baby's initial comprehension that his rage can damage the person he loves creates anxiety about her well-being, but the mother's ability to sustain their connection helps the baby develop the ability to regulate frightening feelings. He learns how to understand and respond to the mental states of the people in his life by creating an internal representation of himself, whose accuracy is impacted by the level of nurturing he receives. This development of the child's psychic reality has lasting implications, empowering the child to manage anxiety when facing challenges, and to feel and contain unpleasant emotions when circumstances call for them.

There are any number of reasons, however, why the mother might not be able to feel her child's discomfort or recognize his needs: the mother may be overly depressed, distracted or distant, or the baby may simply be too active for his needs to be interpreted, or for him to take in or even perceive her loving efforts. Whatever the reason, when mother and infant do not engage in this vital exchange, the effect on the child's psychological development may be significant. His fear remains unrelieved, and the split between good and bad does not heal. Relying on primitive and ineffective tools to manage his anxiety, but still desperate to rid himself of his bad and conflicting feelings that he lacks the ability to integrate, the emotionally uncontained baby continues to project his negative feelings on his surroundings, dependent upon unevolved mechanisms to protect what has become a compensatory idealized image of himself and his inner world. Devoid of ambiguity, and peopled by unreal figures, his world remains simplified, placing parts of his personality at risk.

The relationship between the infant and the outside world establishes a framework that one returns to throughout life, according to Melanie Klein. The child who fails to progress into the process of integration will later face calamitous consequences in adulthood, the signs of which I look for when I am assessing patients in my practice. The infant's unintegrated, split worldview will reappear in adult perspectives that are easily identifiable reflections of the individual's fragmented state of mind. He fills his world with caricatures of evil that he can attack without remorse, seeing himself as victim rather than aggressor or victimizer. Evading accountability for a role he can't recognize, unburdened by any threats to his idealized self-image that a sense of responsibility might bring, his feelings of infallibility flourish, unchallenged by reality in his fantasy world. The adult who is mired in the infant's primitive patterns of division will oversimplify his world by viewing it with black-and-white thinking or friend-or-foe characterizations, or by reducing reality to an epic contest between righteous and evil, good and bad, winners and losers. For decades, I have observed these symptoms of arrested psychological development in my patients. Now we see them in our president, Donald Trump.

Because Trump doesn't say much about his mother in general or her maternal presence in particular, it's hard to imagine him writing or saying anything critical about her mothering style; from what we know about how Trump describes anything and everything else in the world, any criticism of Mary Trump's maternal presence would in his self-centered perspective somehow reflect poorly on him, which he would of course avoid or refuse to do. (It would also open him up for criticism from others, and he always rejected sounding defensive.) Conversely, had she lavished maternal love on her middle son, he would no doubt have let us know that as well—again, likely as a reflection of his lovability.

Instead, Mary Trump is as scarce a presence in Donald Trump's accounts of his life as she is in his contemporaries' memories of Trump family life—or was in his Oval Office photo display until he added her photo to join his father's, which one can imagine was suggested to improve the optics. Writing about his "very traditional" family in *Trump: The Art of the Deal*, Trump describes his mother as "the perfect housewife"—hardly a warm verbal embrace of a son for his mother. Elaborating on that label, he continues, "That didn't mean she sat around playing bridge and talking on the phone. There were five children in all, and besides taking care of us, she cooked and cleaned and darned socks and did charity work at the local hospital." Again, there's nothing about the portrait Trump offers of his mother that indicates he regards her as a loving, nurturing force. (With all those servants, did she really clean and darn socks—or even cook? We'll never know, unless siblings Maryanne, Elizabeth, or Robert speak up.) And, no doubt unintentionally, Donald's remark reveals the implication that perfect housewives have no power—which may shed light on why years later his commencing his affair with Marla Maples coincided with Ivana's beginning to exert her power running a hotel business.

Trump's longest anecdote about his mother is perhaps the most revealing. "Looking back, I realize now that I got some of my sense of showmanship from my mother," he writes. "She always had a flair for the dramatic and the grand." Again, showmanship, drama, and grandeur are hardly the stuff of maternal authenticity that a son might reflect back upon remembering a different kind of mother-son dynamic. When a child is hungry for love he often imitates the remote parent as a way to have that parent inside, as a way of keeping that parent close at hand. It helps growth and development when the child's inner world might otherwise be more barren. At the same time, he might also—and I think this is the case—identify with that quality she *did* possess, i.e., remoteness. He is remote at moments, alternating between being in touch with interviewers and being completely detached. Identification with the parent who causes injury is a defense against expressing open criticism. In Donald's case, I think he identified with each of his parents' most threatening qualities: maternal remoteness and paternal tyrannical demands. Nevertheless, his continuation of the anecdote confirms her lasting impact on him: "I still remember my mother, who is Scottish by birth, sitting in front of the television set to watch Queen Elizabeth's coronation and not budging for an entire day. She was just enthralled by the pomp and circumstance, the whole idea of royalty and glamour. I also remember my father that day, pacing around impatiently. 'For Christ's sake, Mary,' he'd say. 'Enough is enough, turn it off. They're all a bunch of con artists.' My mother didn't even look up. They were total opposites in that sense. My mother loves splendor and magnificence, while my father, who is very down-to-earth, gets excited only by competence and efficiency." What Donald obliquely acknowledged was that his father recognized con artists and did not find them particularly notable or likable.

The anecdote is remarkable for its specificity, which is scarce in Trump's childhood recollections of his mother. Whether it necessarily looms as large in Trump's unconscious as it does in his presentation of his childhood is impossible to know, but it certainly continues the representation of Mary Trump as distracted and self-involved, with the additional element of identifying the "pomp and circumstance" of the royal family as getting her attention when her own family doesn't. More revealing, Trump's including this particular anecdote sets up ongoing themes with an exactness that would be a stretch to ascribe to a first-time memoirist: his mother demonstrating that what gets her attention is very much like what young Donald grew up to try to re-create, even at one point comparing his Trump Tower home to Versailles; and his father speaking the unspeakable truth of the con behind the illusion, at once both affirming and condemning the con artist his son would grow into, putting him on notice that the son could never legitimately or authentically provide the mother what she wants.

Elsewhere in *The Art of the Deal*, Trump offers another clue that his feelings about his mother were largely unconscious. "It's funny," he writes. "My own mother was a housewife all her life. And yet it's turned out that I've hired a lot of women for top jobs, and they've been among my best people. Often, in fact, they are far more effective than the men around them." Beyond the apparent sexism, Trump calls attention to the likelihood that his feelings about his mother remain unconscious with his awkward claim that "and yet it's turned out" that he has hired women for "top" positions despite his mother being a housewife. What one has to do with the other is far from clear; what is clear is the backhanded insult he gives his mother by trying to compliment his female employees. There is something here about ownership as well, that the women working for him are *his* best people. Again it is about function, not about other qualities. His mother sounds like she was respected—something his father demanded from his children—and at the same time seen either as not relevant or, at best, as a kind of servant herself. Unconsciously this reinforces the child's denial of dependency, especially denial of a need for warmth, affection, and love. Rather, the mother here is virtually indistinguishable from housekeeper, more a function than a person. Howard Stern pointed out something similar after Trump told him that marrying Melania turned his business fortunes around. Stern said, "You talk like she's a lucky charm, not a person."

His employees aren't the only women in Trump's life who he compares to his mother. "Part of the problem I've had with women has been in having to compare them to my incredible mother, Mary Trump," Trump writes in *The Art of the Comeback*. "My mother is smart as hell." Close observers of Trump are not surprised to hear him find his mother *smart* and *incredible*, because rating people is such a common defense for him, one that likely goes back to early childhood efforts to manage the anxiety of uncertainty by asserting control over one's world by judging others. But smart and incredible are of course not the same as loving, connecting, and maternal. The most specific aspect of this particular comparison of other women to his mother is of course the result—the *problem* he has with women.

The *Art of the Comeback* quote is indicative of the imprecision with which Trump speaks or writes when he actually does talk about his mother. Kruse catalogs many of the platitudes Trump has evoked in discussing his mother, noting that "in interviews over the past several decades, the president has called her 'fantastic' and 'tremendous' and 'very warm'—'a homemaker' who 'loved it.'" Kruse adds that Trump told Martha Stewart on her television show that his mother "used to do a great job" with her meat loaf; on his beloved Twitter, Trump referred to his mother simply as "a wonderful person" and "a great beauty." And on the 2016 campaign trail, Kruse notes, Trump followed a claim that "nobody respects women more than [him]," with the hollow claim that the "greatest person ever was my mother. Believe me, the greatest." Between the wild claim about his respect for women and his familiar "believe me" entreaty, Trump is sending distinct signals that whatever he says about his mother is different from—if not opposite to—how he really feels, or at least how he also feels.

Kruse also cites generic words of maternal wisdom that Trump put in front of his Twitter followers no fewer than seven times in two years: "Advice from my mother, Mary MacLeod Trump: Trust in God and be true to yourself." Is it too much sophistry on my part to infer that being true to yourself is the same as being true to God, i.e., that he is God? Kruse also cites a *Sunday Times* of London interview in which Trump told the reporter, "The values she gave to me were strong values.... I wish I could have picked up all of them, but I didn't, obviously." This moment of humility and seeming self-reflection raises the question of which of his mother's values he was referring to. One also wonders whether he ignored them or rejected them actively—or if he was thinking of his mother's equally unguarded and almost certainly haunting moment of reflection in the 1990 pages of *Vanity Fair*, where it was reported that she'd once asked her daughter-in-law Ivana, "What kind of son have I created?"

IT WAS IN ANOTHER discussion of his mother's values that Trump offered some of the most vivid, and almost certainly unintentional, glimpses into his interior life. In a Q&A in the final pages of his 2007 self-help tome, *Think Big: Make It Happen in Business and Life*, Trump actually acknowledges that his upbringing—particularly his relationship with his father—left him with a level of mental health that was something shy of ideal, letting slip that he regards himself as "screwed up." In answer to the question of the best advice that his parents gave him growing up, Trump responds: "They gave me different advice. My mother was a wife who was really a great homemaker. She always said, 'Be happy!' She wanted me to be happy. My father understood me more and he said, 'I want you to be successful.' He was a very driven kind of guy. That's why I'm so screwed up, because I had a father that pushed me pretty hard. My father was a tough man, but he was a good man. He was a kind man, and he would tell me to always do something that you love. Now I'm happy, so I ended up doing what both of my parents wanted me to do." He revealed more self-awareness than we usually see from him. While not revealing a moral compass, he does seem to "get" what his parents were about. He needed immediately to backpedal from what he wrote about his father—rather than continue to elaborate on how that "tough man" affected him—and what things his father was particularly tough about.

As we've seen before, Trump reveals more than intended in his uncharacteristically candid moment of self-awareness. Perhaps most telling is the admission that his father "understood [him] more"—which suggests of course that his mother "understood" him less. Trump expressed a similar sentiment to biographer Tim O'Brien, to whom he made the impossible claim, "My father was more directly related to me." Perhaps Trump has had at least some awareness of his disregard for his mother; Kruse quotes a 1992 interview with Charlie Rose in which Trump says, "One of my attorneys said, 'Always count on your mother.' Now, you know, I maybe took advantage of my mother. I never appreciated her as much. . . ."

A child who doesn't feel understood by or related to his mother grows into adulthood with his psychological development significantly disadvantaged. So much of Trump's recognizable pathology—the familiar grandiosity, the need for reassurance that he's well loved and seen as extraordinarily successful, and the complex process of not feeling understood—compromises one's ability to understand others. At one level it leads to empathic failure. At another level, it has helped Trump hone his powerful capacity to "read" other people—also a compensation for not having been read by his own mother. I think that the only person in Trump's life who really knew him—other than his first wife, Ivana—was his father. He saw his son's great strength as well as his comfort with delinquency, which can be traced to an early breakdown in the mother-son connection.

If Mary Trump were indeed as absent from the infant Donald's formative interactions with his mother as she was reportedly from the rest of his childhood—and remains relatively absent from his memory and from his perspective—then many of his contemporary attitudes can be read as adult expressions of deeply ingrained, lifelong limitations to his ability to embrace empathy, ambivalence, and complexity. A child needs to be confident that he is loved so he can risk hating the very person who loves him. That makes it safe enough to express the full range of feelings. If not, one retreats from complexity and nuance, and even from feeling ambivalence. This also has to do with Trump's memory—he can say something positive one day and negative the next day about the same person. It's harder for him to do so simultaneously, unless he's trying to make up for criticizing someone who reminds him of his father. Then there is good on both sides.

Even Trump's obsession with image can be traced back to infancy. In the normal, healthy dynamic, the baby looks into his mother's eyes as she feeds him at the bottle or breast. He can see himself reflected in those eyes, feeling his love reverberate with hers. They share that in a "harmonious mix-up" described by many psychoanalysts observing mother-infant relationships in the early months.

But sometimes this vital connection isn't sufficiently developed—because the mother is distracted, for example, or because the child is too jumpy to take her gaze—and the infant who didn't get enough of his mother's attention grows into an adult who hungers for attention from others. It's easy to see how this dynamic would have evolved between Donald and his disengaged mother. The depth of his current need for attention and affirmation makes more sense when understood as an adult expression of a lifelong craving with roots in the earliest years of childhood.

An inconsistent bond between mother and infant leads to an adult inability to internalize parental love enough to build genuine self-esteem. Trump's deficit of healthy self-esteem paradoxically thus renders him dependent upon the attention of others—particularly the media, whose attention he craves to heal the loss of his mother's childhood gaze. These psychological stakes contribute to a relationship between Trump and the media that is beyond his control and his capacity to break away from. Unable to accept or acknowledge his deep psychological need for their admiring, affirming, or soothing gaze, he bridles against his dependency on the media, denying the legitimacy or importance of the press. When the media offer an unadmiring reflection, he experiences their criticism as their asserting a level of autonomy he knows he doesn't himself possess. It activates the early disharmony Trump experienced with his mother, so he responds with resentment, dismissal, and even threats. He is so dependent on the press that he must reassure himself that the opposite is true, and fights back against anything that challenges his denial.

Trump's overreaction to his treatment in the media brings to mind another critical developmental stage in the life of the infant. In healthy development, at some point after the infant has begun to internalize the affirming power of his mother's gaze, he comes face-to-face with the power of the gaze of another—himself. French psychoanalyst Jacques Lacan described the "mirror stage" in which the infant comes into contact with his own reflection. What the infant sees in the mirror, however, appears to possess more integration and self-control than he knows or physically experiences in his chaotic existence as an infant. The reflected image establishes an ideal version of the self that the individual will typically spend a lifetime pursuing—always inevitably reminding himself of the frustrating distance between the real and ideal selves whenever he repeatedly and inevitably falls short.

The infant who is confronting his own reflection without the empowering benefit of regularly receiving and returning his mother's loving gaze will have a harder time confronting the gap between his real and ideal selves—a gap that will be experienced as being more pronounced by an infant with restless, hyperactive tendencies, which we'll see that Donald Trump manifested in his childhood. Donald's challenges navigating the lifelong process of knowing where to place his ideal self became even more difficult in adulthood when his ideal self was broadcast into millions of homes at a time. He soon realized that the Donald Trump reality-show character was far more successful than the man who was playing him on television. (One way to think about this is that on *The Apprentice*, Donald was able to become his ideal self, to claim it as if it were really his to have, his to be.) His needy bravado makes this harder to assess, because he wants reassurance far too often. But at the same time his numerous daily tweets on many different subjects reflect a grandiose, confident fantasy that as president he can say and do whatever he wants to, whenever he wants. He is unselfconscious in those tweets, much like a young teenager who is full of himself and his power in the world—not self-conscious on one level, but needing to look in the mirror regularly as well, to reaffirm his grandeur.

These days, however, when Donald Trump looks into the mirror, he also sees something else entirely. As online commenters enthusiastically reported in 2017, and as anyone familiar with Mary Trump's personal style already knew, Donald Trump looks into the mirror and sees . . . his mother. Or, at least, his mother's hair. Any observer can instantly understand that Donald Trump's hair doesn't have to look the way it does—and wouldn't, in fact, without great forethought and effort. As enterprising Internet sleuths made very public last year, with a few pictures that spoke thousands of words, Donald Trump's hairstyle shares an assertive disregard for both gravity and natural color with the style his mother wore. The unasked question—*Hey, what's with the hair?*—that vied to be the opening salvo of a hypothetical therapy session with Trump is perhaps more effectively framed to ask: Why does Trump wear his hair so similar to the parent he felt didn't understand him? Is he still hoping to re-create the maternal gaze he missed as an infant? Or is this just the latest of Donald Trump's decisions crafted to elicit his father's hard-won support? As we'll see, Donald has a long history of trying to please his father—with very mixed results.

Chapter Two

FATHER

Mismanagement and grief:
We must suffer them all again.

—*W. H. Auden*

My father taught me everything I know, and he would understand what I'm about to say," Donald Trump told a roomful of mourners at his father's wake. "I'm developing a great building on Riverside Boulevard called Trump Place. It's a wonderful project." In what passed in Donald's mind as an appropriate eulogy from a son for his father, he then proceeded to list some of his own projects—the Grand Hyatt, Trump Tower, Trump Plaza, Trump Taj Mahal, Trump's Castle—before acknowledging that his father had "passed down Donald's most treasured asset," write Michael Kranish and Marc Fisher in their book *Trump Revealed*, "the emblem of all his accomplishments: the Trump name. 'The name just sells,' Donald was quoted as saying."

No less of a Trump expert than the late gossip columnist

Liz Smith, writes Michael D'Antonio in his book *The Truth About Trump*, observed that Trump is "often ruled by the needy child who resides in his psyche." Recounting a list of his own accomplishments while ostensibly eulogizing his father—and claiming his father would understand—Trump's needy inner child was at that moment perhaps never needier, or at least never more evident. Donald Trump had one last opportunity to solicit the approval he had most needed and aggressively pursued—his father's—and he saw no disrespect in making the moment about him in order to do so. In fact, he claimed, his father would understand what he was doing, and why.

Donald referred to his father as his "best friend," "a very difficult guy," and "a great teacher for me." Clearly, Fred Trump was the most influential person in Donald's life. He followed in his father's footsteps professionally, went into the family business, and emulated at least some of his business practices on his path to success. More than anyone else, Donald sought to impress his father, prove himself to him, and ultimately surpass him. Donald was of course financially indebted to his father, for the still-unspecified share of the family fortune Fred gave to his son to help get him started, and for the other sums Fred gave Donald when he needed financial rescue.

At the same time, however, Donald describes a father-son dynamic that is no warmer than the relationship he has reported with his mother, and the limits of Fred's availability and presence as a father have been widely reported. Donald openly defied and rebuked some of the business practices his father taught him. And while telling his son that he was "a king," it was his father who essentially exiled Donald from the family, sending him to military school, imposing strict and sudden order on what was becoming an increasingly disorderly youth, a profound disruption that inevitably reverberated in the years that followed. Donald was exiled because Fred understood full well that he could no longer control his son without help, and that he required the services of the New York Military Academy. Interestingly, at the time of his exile, Donald was the same age that Fred was when his father died, a reminder that Fred lacked the experience of witnessing fatherly help during his own adolescence. It was the NYMA that fathered Donald when Fred realized he couldn't. Fred recognized his son's delinquency; he knew that Donald needed stricter limits than a regular school atmosphere could set, no matter how much Fred Sr. laid down the law at home.

"We had a relationship that was almost businesslike," Trump writes of his father in *The Art of the Deal*. "I sometimes wonder if we'd have gotten along so well if I hadn't been as business-oriented as I am." Of course, a businesslike father-son dynamic is inevitably short on the nurturing, affection, and love for which a son might typically look to his father. As we'll see, however, that "businesslike" relationship was characterized by a variety of other factors that still resonate today.

As Donald Trump well knows, he owes his personal fortune to his father's and grandfather's unethical business practices that exploited the aspirations of an economic class that would now qualify as his voter base. Friedrich Trump, Donald's grandfather, made his initial fortune as the proprietor of brothels catering to prospectors during the Klondike Gold Rush, discovering that he could make more money meeting the baser instincts of the get-rich-quick fortune hunters than by doing the actual hard work of mining, a fact Trump never points out when pandering to the coal miners whose votes he wants. "As a rogue entrepreneur," David Cay Johnston writes of Donald's grandfather, "Friedrich cast a century-long shadow over the Trump family with his passion for money and the flouting of legal niceties—such as erecting buildings on land he did not own." Johnston posits that the lesson was not lost on Donald, who would later proudly recount several business successes that hinged on his representing that he owned land that he had yet to acquire. "Building on land he did not own," writes Johnston, "foreshadowed the terms under which his grandson Donald would acquire the Florida mansion Mar-a-Lago: with a mortgage that Chase Bank agreed in writing not to record at the courthouse."

Trump also never mentions a personal fact that would be relevant in any discussions of border security: namely, his grandfather was, in Kranish and Fisher's account, "an illegal emigrant." After making his fortune in America, Friedrich Trump attempted a permanent return to his German homeland with his homesick wife and daughter, but the terms under which he had left Germany earlier came back to haunt him. "Friedrich's departure ran afoul of German law," they write. "A three-year stint of military service was mandatory, and to emigrate, boys of conscription age had to get permission. The young barber didn't do so, resulting in a questionable status that would undermine any future prospect of return." The German officials "asked why [Friedrich] Trump hadn't come back sooner to perform his military service. To them, he looked like a draft dodger." Trump was ultimately the beneficiary of "US immigration law at the time granted Germans preferred status; they were viewed as having the proper white European ethnic stock and an industrious nature."

When Friedrich returned to the US with his family, he started a thriving construction business in Queens, where he would bring his young son Fred along to construction sites. Friedrich died suddenly in the 1918 Spanish flu pandemic, just days after he turned forty-nine. Some in the family believed his death was hastened by alcoholism; the family lost most of its fortune and it fell upon young Fred to learn the construction trade. He started a business with his mother, E. Trump and Son, in time to take advantage of the 1920s building boom in Brooklyn and Queens—fueled in part by civic-funded infrastructure improvements that turned the outer boroughs into accessible housing options for Manhattan workers. The Trumps lost everything again when E. Trump and Son went out of business during the Depression, but Fred was back in business and well on his way to making another fortune by the time he met and married Mary Ann MacLeod in 1936, when he was thirty-one.

Although Donald would eventually describe his father as a self-made man, a classic American success story, one of the secrets to Fred Trump's success during the Depression was his willingness and ability to take advantage of others' misfortune. "Trump found opportunity in gloom," write Kranish and Fisher. "When a mortgage firm called Lehrenkrauss & Co. was broken up amid charges of fraud, Trump and a partner scooped up a subsidiary that held title to many distressed properties. Trump used that information to buy houses facing foreclosure, expanding his real estate holdings with properties bought on the cheap from people who had little choice other than to sell."

Later, with World War II on the horizon, "Trump boasted that the threat of combat had helped business," write Kranish and Fisher. "'In the event of war, I believe that the profit will be quicker and larger,' Trump said, trying to gin up sales. The remark might have seemed impolitic, but it proved correct, at least for his company." A bigger boon awaited after the war, when returning veterans' dreams of homeownership were placed within reach through generous federal loan programs. "Although Fred boasted that he was a self-made man," writes Trump biographer Harry Hurt III in his book *Lost Tycoon: The Many Lives of Donald J. Trump*, "he laid the foundations of the Trump fortune with Federal Housing Administration loans." Trump's success at exploiting loopholes to game the

FHA system for personal profit landed him in trouble in 1954, when he was called to testify before a US Senate committee "to answer for $4 million in windfall profits he took from a government housing program for war veterans," explain Kranish and Fisher. And it was in that setting, as Fred Trump explained a complex but ultimately legal scheme for minimizing the appearance of profits, that Congress heard its first—albeit oblique—reference to Donald Trump, as one of the Trump children for whom Fred had created a trust that officially owned and leased out the land on which he had built the veterans' housing.

By this point Donald was eight years old, ensconced in a home that Fred had built on a double-sized lot to resemble a Southern plantation (complete with columns and lawn jockeys), and—in the words of biographer D'Antonio—already exhibiting "problem-child behavior." D'Antonio cites tales of "erasers hurled at teachers and cake flung at birthday parties" as well as the possibly apocryphal story of the second-grade Trump punching a music teacher hard enough to give him a black eye, because Trump "didn't think he knew anything about music." Kranish and Fisher offer tales of Donald's life in the neighborhood, where, "when a neighbor's ball accidentally bounced into the Trumps' spacious backyard," they write, "young Donald growled, 'I'm going to tell my dad; I'm going to call the police.'" They also recount a troubling incident from another former neighbor, Dennis Burnham, who "grew up a few doors away from the Trumps," they write. "When he was a toddler, his mother placed him in a backyard playpen. Once, after going inside for a few minutes, she returned to find that little Donald—five or six at the time—had wandered over and was throwing rocks at her son, Burnham said." Fast-forward to the day after the Marjory Stoneman Douglas High School murders, President Trump—now grown-up Donny—tweeted, "So many signs that the Florida shooter was mentally disturbed, even expelled from school for bad and erratic behavior. Neighbors and classmates knew he was a big problem. Must always report such instances to authorities, again and again!" Trump has a continuous need to evoke past experiences and use them to interpret present events, while unconsciously sending the message that he compulsively blames others—this time "neighbors and classmates" who didn't do enough. It's as if he says he'll never stop his own bad behavior—it's up to others to do it, and if they don't, it's their fault if he gets away with delinquency.

Within the family, Kranish and Fisher write, "Donald spent the most time with Robert, his little brother, a quiet, sensitive youngster and easy prey for an aggressive older sibling." Two years Donald's junior, Robert appears in one of the few stories that Donald tells of his childhood. "As an adult, Donald liked to tell the story of when he appropriated Robert's building blocks for his own and glued them together because he was so pleased with what he had made," they write. "'And that was the end of Robert's blocks,' Donald recalled."

A child exhibiting this kind of behavior today could be the

recipient of some outside therapeutic assistance, or might get reported to authorities, depending on whose toddler was being pelted in his playpen. As we go to press, Trump has become the authority who turns a cold shoulder to immigrant children locked in cages. He would almost certainly be labeled a bully. Those behaviors presaged Trump's persisting hatred of weakness in others—when he was a toddler he must have been frightened after his mother suddenly abandoned him to give birth to Robert before requiring extended hospital care for herself. Soon Donald equated being frightened with weakness. Bullies attack children or other seemingly weak people with added venom, both instilling fear at one level and also expressing their unconscious contempt for any weakness that reminds them of themselves. A toddler in a playpen is defenseless, trapped the way Donald felt as a young child—trapped in his own home and at the whim of his father without any protection we can identify yet. When Dennis Burnham was in that playpen he was about the same age Donald was when his mother went to the hospital to give birth to Robert and then to almost die. Donald must have felt trapped at that time, and maybe very frightened to lose his already somewhat disengaged mother in such a sudden and dramatic way. Seeing that little boy next door a few years later was a perfect source of temptation for Donald's displaced self-hatred, which he converted into projected contempt. The bully is first driven by what Anna Freud called "identification with the aggressor," in this case Donald's identification with his father. But in this story, what's central was his hatred of a helpless toddler—someone Donald would now call "a loser"—who represents his own self-hatred at having once been frightened and vulnerable.

Donald was a big kid, though he was more comfortable pushing around those much smaller than he was. Bullies often develop their aggressive tendencies in response to a powerful father. The son of a powerful father may transform his fear of his father into a fear of bullies—which in turn is transformed into a drive to become a bully himself, managing his fear of his father by exaggerating his identification with the power and aggression he fears.

Fred Trump was absent from home when he was working, which was often—so often that Donald could best see his father by being taken to a work site. And when Fred Trump was home his word was everything, and all the children fell into line—that is, until he discovered that Donald was secretly defiant. What Fred remembered of his own father is not known, but we know that the father typically plays a central role in his children's concept of manhood, leading to an internal image of paternal power and masculinity that the son both wants and fears. Yearning mixed with fear created Donald's image of manhood, as did Fred's rejection of sentimentality and insistence on being properly dressed at all times. Fred Sr. demanded respect for himself and the appearance of respectability for his son (as when he demanded that Donald not bring Marla Maples to the opening of the Trump Taj Mahal).

At school young Donald was no better. He was such a

disciplinary problem that Kranish and Fisher report that he "spent enough time in detention that his friends nicknamed the punishment DTs—for 'Donny Trumps.'" They report teachers describing him as "headstrong," "surly," "determined," "a pain," and even "a little shit"—the latter coming from a teacher who told them, "There are certain kids that need attention all the time. He was one of those." Explaining his school record to Kranish and Fisher, Trump said his primary focus was "creating mischief because, for some reason, I liked to stir things up and I liked to test people. . . . It wasn't malicious so much as it was aggressive." He used the same approach to "Little Rocket Man," to give the appearance of being aggressive and tough. The problem is that both men, still children at heart, are armed with nuclear weapons. He likes threatening people, giving the impression of toughness and reminding everyone that he's not a pushover. He also said, "What separates the winners from the losers is how a person reacts to each new twist of fate." Throwing rocks at the confined toddler is a delayed reaction to the twist of fate he suffered two years earlier when his mother was sent away.

Donald Trump's childhood behavior is characteristic of children in a family like the Trumps of Donald's youth, where the father is powerful but absent. Left to form their own rules of behavior, children in such circumstances develop their own ways of managing their internal worlds. (This is not always the case, as a child may internalize the father's tyranny and become like him, thus experiencing the father as unconsciously present, not missed.) Psychologically, a child needs the presence of a parent—or both parents—to help him develop an internal coherent sense of self. Fred Trump was an absent presence—a father inconsistently around but whose strict authoritarian parenting was always present. What was absent was paternal praise. As a result, young Donald's innate aggression and impulsive behaviors were not met with the level of active paternal presence that could have helped modify them. Instead, his behavior was a caricature of his dominant father. When an aggressive child lacks a parent attuned to his rage and frustration, his efforts to be more internally balanced will be compromised. He will learn to love only himself—and most likely to hate parental figures, particularly those with the kind of limit-setting qualities that would make him feel controlled. A more structured upbringing, however, could have helped him change the way he defined himself.

The absence of the father has a particularly pronounced effect on the son's development involving aggression—how to handle his own and others', and how to recognize it in others and in himself. All sons at some point, early in psychic development, need to confront their fathers. When the father is present, the son typically projects his aggression onto the father, and then fears the father based on this projection. The son competes or fights with the father and then repairs the damage done—a variation on the mother-infant dynamic of break-and-repair that helps the son learn how to modulate his aggression. The son benefits further by witnessing the father model healthy aggression, as when one parent stands up to the other, when the father sets limits on the children, or when he stands up to someone. As this process repeats itself over time, the son internalizes his love and rage toward the father. The process is a replay of the shift in mental positions—the son at first experiencing having a good and bad daddy, one who he loves and one who he fears. The coming together of those two internal fathers, their integration into self, is more difficult when the material (real) father is not present.

A son who lacks or loses his father at a young age often grows up with what Harvard psychoanalyst James Herzog identified as "father hunger," a deep yearning to get close to a father who isn't there, that can be covered over or expressed in indirect ways. Father hunger often precipitates the son's search for a male authority figure who values and admires him in a way that resembles a dynamic missing from the father-son relationship. Young Donald was likely vulnerable to such yearning due to the distant nature of his connection with his father. In early adolescence, however, Trump's issues with his father would be suddenly and significantly escalated when his father stepped in to try to address his middle son's unmanageable (or at least unmanaged) aggression—in a move with unforeseeable psychological repercussions that continue to reverberate today, now with global consequences.

Gwenda Blair talked to one of Trump's classmates from the

Kew-Forest School, who told her that Donald and his best friend, Peter Brant, "really pushed the limits in terms of authority and what they could get away with." Decades later, it's easy to interpret Trump's behavior as indicating that challenging authority is now his main goal. Trump's aversion to rules and regulations can be interpreted as fear of castration and shaming, or a deep need to be omnipotent—to be the ultimate authority.

Blair details the famous story of the incident that led to Trump's being sent to New York Military Academy after seventh grade. "One of the things [Donald and Peter] liked to do best was ride the subway into Manhattan on Saturdays and go to a magic store at West 49th Street and Broadway. There they bought stink bombs and smoke bombs and plastic vomit. Another favorite was hot peppered gum, which they gave to unsuspecting schoolmates. After seeing *West Side Story*, they became fascinated with switchblades. 'A switchblade knife was an exciting thing for an eleven-year-old to have,' Peter said. 'We bought a little one, then a bigger one, and finally we were up to an eleven-inch knife. There was nothing bad in it, we just wanted to play Land [a game with knives they invented] and listen to the noise of flicking the blade.'"

In Trump's preteen worldview, Manhattan represented the forbidden land—which he has been trying to conquer ever since. As an adolescent who believed in magic—at least enough to go to the magic store—and lived in a fantasy world of omnipotence, sneaking into Manhattan without being discovered also involves an unconscious fantasy of being invisible. And he was clearly drawn to the *West Side Story* image of outlaw rivalries settled through violence, with weapons he could bring back home to Queens, where he bullied his weaker friends (and felt like Superman internally). Even better, the progression of the original smaller weapon getting bigger with each conquest is clearly a phallic idea, rooted in the Oedipal desire to get big enough to defeat the father. As president, Donald Trump finally turned his back on *West Side Story*, exchanging switchblades for paper towels he threw at hurricane-ravaged Puerto Ricans.

Discovering the switchblades and the secret Manhattan trips, writes Blair, was "the last straw" for a Fred Trump "already disturbed by the reports he received about Donald's behavior in the classroom" at the school where he (Fred) served as a trustee, as well as in Sunday school and in youth group. Donald wasn't only out of control; he was making his father look bad as he acted out against a variety of authoritative institutions. His punishment—being banished from the family home and exiled to military school—made it dramatically, painfully clear to Donald who held the power in his dynamic with his father. (He also knew that his father understood him and wouldn't tolerate this kind of impulsive disobedience. One notes that it wasn't the incident of Donny punching his teacher that precipitated his being sent away—it was his secretly disobeying his father. It's also true that amassing a collection of knives by an impulsive son could make even an unconsciously Oedipally-minded father uneasy.)

Kranish and Fisher's version of the discovery of the knife

collection makes clear that it was the fathers who took the action—and Donald's father more than Peter's: "Near the end of seventh grade, Fred discovered Donald's cache of knives. Fred called Peter's father, who found his own son's collection. The parents were infuriated to learn about the youngers' trips to the city. . . . Fred Trump, alarmed by how his son was evolving, decided Donald needed a radical change." Fred Trump understood that his son was out of control, but now also that he could endanger his own family by using his hidden knife collection.

In making the decision to send him to NYMA, Fred was admitting to himself that he couldn't cope; by actually facing the fact of not being able to cope—instead of continuously trying to cope but failing, like all the detentions Donny received at school—Fred quite possibly established himself as the first and perhaps only person who had ever honestly dealt with Donald. He was the one person who set limits that Donald obeyed (after his delinquent Manhattan behavior was discovered). True, there were lawyers and businessmen who refused to negotiate with him over the years, but nobody tried to change his behavior by exiling him. Setting limits with destructive adolescents is always the first step in setting up treatment, and points to the obvious—if unlikely—first step in dealing with the still-destructive President Trump.

Remarkably, Donald didn't tell Peter of his punishment. "In the months before eighth grade was to begin," Kranish and Fisher write, "Donald seemed to vanish. Peter heard from a friend that his buddy would be attending another school. When Peter telephoned him, Donald, his voice thick with de-jection," told him he was being sent away to NYMA. The dis-ruption was so severe that young Donald couldn't bring himself to talk about it voluntarily.

Before the school year started, Donald was sent for one last time to summer camp, where he gave the first-known expres-sion to what would become his most visible coping mechanism, now familiar the world over. In previous years, Donald's older brother, Fred Jr., had gotten in trouble at the same camp for sneaking off campus and into town; Donald, Blair writes, "learned from his brother's experience" and instead "concen-trated on doing only what he wanted to do around camp." Blair quotes one of the camp owners' son's observation that the "or-nery" young Trump "tried to get out of activities whenever he could" and "figured out all the angles." One "safe outlet," re-ports Blair, "was to paint 'Don Trump 59' inside the door of his cabin. Whenever camp got to him, he could lie down on his bunk and look over at the sight of his own name." Of course, Trump has been labeling buildings with his name to show the world that he was not going to make the same mistakes as his brother ever since, and the world will never be the same.

BEHIND THE EFFORT THAT ultimately remade the world in Trump's name was an unconscious desire to remake his own world. One narcissistic defense against perceptions of attack, called the "psychic retreat," is observed when an individual withdraws into total self-love and interacts even less with others. He becomes a rule maker overtly and a rule breaker only when it is safe. The rest of the time he wraps himself in the family name for protection. He would be hard to work with clinically because of that powerful defense. And it helps us see how he wraps himself up inside Trump Tower—living *inside* his own name. He hasn't changed since camp—and his behavior protects him from attack and punishment when he's at risk. And he can continue his ambitious drive for money and power as he sees fit.

A full-blown psychic retreat freezes the personality and blocks it from changing and developing or maturing over time. It is an inner narcissistic structure created to protect the person from anxieties caused by perceptions of threats both external— such as menacing parents or family members—and internal— such as fears of dependency and vulnerability, or violent and destructive impulses. The retreat offers the individual a safe psychic space from which there is no need to emerge unless one is coaxed out, or there is a demand to interact with the world— after which the individual quickly returns to his safe space to assuage his anxiety.

The line from Trump's name painted on his camp cabin door to Trump Tower and other Trump-labeled edifices ex- tends all the way to Fox News, which President Trump is known to have made his favorite and trusted companion inside his psychic retreat. But the psychic retreat ultimately is unconscious, and mentally Trump builds an inner wall against symbolic intruders that is echoed by the wall he promises to build on the Mexican border. So great are his fears of persecutors, however, that he must remain on the alert at all times, bingeing on cable news, both threatening and reassuring, and restricting his sleep to a minimal number of hours.

There are elements of this function in all of us: many of us retreat from the threats of our divided world into the relative unity of cable news—albeit different channels. But most of us don't spend as much time in our psychic retreats as Trump does. Trump makes that retreat palpable, as he literally keeps away from others while watching *Fox & Friends* on Fox News every morning. He had a similar retreat in Trump Tower—so his retreats are internal as well as concretely real. I think the same applies to his obsession with the border wall—it is the physical representation of an internal process that is integral to his psychic retreat. He walls off unpleasant and threatening ideas.

In extreme instances, an individual with a well-constructed internal retreat is driven to avoid not only having meaningful contact with other people, but also to evade simply facing reality because it makes him too anxious. While the external expression of a well-constructed psychic retreat can have the appearance of strength and power, observers may intuitively understand that the construction was rooted in weakness, fear, anxiety, and the need to retreat as well as to reassure himself of both his power and his very existence. One wonders if the more intuitive members of the Republican caucus who enable Trump may sense this and opt not to criticize or turn against him not only out of fear of retaliation—which is a legitimate fear—but also out of an unconscious sense of his fragility lurking behind the retreat, an awareness that someone so vigorously protected might not withstand direct confrontation and could collapse into multiple personality fragments.

Blair describes NYMA as an almost magical solution for young Donald: "For the first time, Donald was in a place that encouraged and channeled competitiveness and aggression instead of tamping it down," she writes. "At last Donald was in a place where winning really mattered, and he poured himself into doing better than everyone else at everything." While transformation of anxiety isn't exactly the same as sublimation, the structure of NYMA clearly set limits on young Donald that allowed him to at least transform his anxiety into something less destructive without undoing its basic aim—to dominate and win. His destructiveness remained, but could be drawn upon and focused when necessary—perhaps made even more powerful by the removal of the scattered quality of his disruptive behavior that preceded his being sent away.

NYMA landed Donald in a "system of hierarchy and authoritarian discipline," writes D'Antonio, where the faculty, "many veterans of World War II, governed with physical and psychological brutality." Some of Donald's classmates arrived with a keener familiarity with the brutality of the world than could be expected from a rich real estate developer's son from Queens. "At NYMA," D'Antonio writes, "the corps of cadets included sons of mafia figures and boys whose fathers served Latin American dictators." It's not a stretch to see that part of NYMA's function was to structure tendencies of competitiveness and aggression that boys observed in and copied from their fathers—who may or may not have appreciated seeing those characteristics mirrored in their sons. The student body certainly embraced a culture of violence; D'Antonio notes that "in Donald's senior year, the ritual hazing at the school got so bad that a junior-level student was hospitalized after an upperclassman whipped him with a heavy chain." D'Antonio concludes, "In addition to confirming that bullying was the way of the world, NYMA reinforced for Trump the idea that competition and winning was everything."

In Blair's telling, the NYMA redirection of Trump's competitiveness was only partially successful. Blair reports that Trump's first-year roommate, Ted Levine, observed that Donald, though liked, "never, never had truly close friends" and "didn't bond with anyone," which Levine attributed to his being "too competitive, and with a friend you don't always compete. It was like he had this defensive wall around him, and he wouldn't let anyone get close. He didn't distrust everybody, but he didn't trust them, either." Levine identifies an attribute that has characterized Trump's interactions ever since; because he's unable to differentiate people from one another, his vision of everything being about either winning or losing has dominated his life.

Even within his family life, he was competitive in his identification with his father in business and also with his role in the family. His family does seem to get the only pass in terms of the trust issue that Blair cites Levine noting: Trump is still so paranoid that if someone goes against him at all, even if it's a person he selected, he distances himself quickly and attacks when he deems it necessary, demonstrating that trust is provisional for him, unless it's within the family.

Levine's observations of military-school-era Trump essentially describe a narcissist wrapped up in his psychic retreat, where he was free to enjoy omnipotent fantasies and think about whatever he wished. His self-imposed isolation left him alone with his grandiose musings. Wrapped up in a bubble that was well cushioned by wealth and fantasies of being a future business tycoon, he was able to cultivate his fantasies of power and superiority.

The one person who was able to pierce the bubble at NYMA was Coach Ted Dobias, who told Blair that Trump "caught my eye right away because he was so aggressive but so coachable." What made him so appealing to Dobias, he told Blair, was that he "was very sure of himself, but he also listened." Dobias also recognized Trump's natural athletic ability, and coached him to distinguished records in several sports. The only black mark on Trump's NYMA athletic career was his suddenly quitting the football team in junior year, which earned him the enmity of some of his classmates. According to Kranish and Fisher, Trump abruptly left the team because "he didn't like the head coach, and the feeling was apparently mutual." Levine theorized to Kranish and Fisher that "the coach was nasty to him," and Trump "got personally abused by authority and was not appreciated." Otherwise his competitive spirit prevailed; Dobias told D'Antonio that "Trump had to be first at everything, including first in line at the chow hall." Now as president, Donald Trump elbows out other NATO leaders to get center spot in their group photo.

One former roommate told Blair that the military environment was "what Donald seemed to love most" about NYMA. "Far from being daunted by the strict discipline," Blair writes, "Donald seemed to welcome being in a place with clear-cut parameters, a place where he could focus on figuring out how to come out on top and get what he wanted." That description hardly comes as a surprise to anyone who observed his emphasis on winning during the 2016 campaign. But the stated objective of the win doesn't identify the unconscious goal for a person with Trump's pathology, which is, quite simply, calm.

Trump no doubt did respond well to the "clear-cut parameters" that NYMA offered, but in young Donald's case it wasn't simply controlling random aggression that mattered; the purpose of his aggression in the first place was to manage incessant internal anxiety—anxiety about falling apart or fragmenting. The discharge of aggression helped make him less anxious—but it never deals directly with its source. All Trump's attacks on others—past and current—revolve around managing anxiety; winning makes for an attainable goal, but the unconscious goal of calm is impossible. Trapped as he is on a psychic treadmill in pursuit of an unattainable objective, his falling short of the goal of releasing his anxiety causes more anxiety, which fuels itself into the now-familiar constant escalation of need we still see today.

Donald's quitting the football team suggests that on some level he knew that the psychic retreat he created for himself within the structure of NYMA was flawed: as well wrapped as he was inside his unconscious retreat, he sensed his anxiety rising and knew enough simply to leave. As even a cursory review of Trump's career makes clear, the solution of simply leaving became familiar to him: the projects he completed are far outnumbered by those he abandoned. Now he is wrapped up in that great American tradition of the presidency, and his unspoken source of comfort is that he knows—when he is criticized or facing tough and substantive discussions that require detailed policy knowledge and are not about winning or losing—that he can easily walk away. In anticipation of his meeting with Kim Jong Un, for example, Trump announced that if he didn't like the proceedings he'd just leave.

One thing that Donald could not walk away from, however, was NYMA; no matter how well he took to its environment of controlled savagery, Trump knew he could never leave, and that he had his father to thank (or blame) for the restrictions on his freedom. Lest Donald forget who sent him there, Fred regularly visited his son at NYMA, more often than most fathers. The visits served as clear reminders of the power dynamic between father and son. As D'Antonio notes, Dobias "recalled that his father 'was really tough on the kid. He was very German.'" Coming from a World War II veteran, that was certainly no compliment—regardless of whether Dobias knew that in the years after the war Fred Trump actively tried to hide his German roots, falsely claiming to be of Swedish heritage, a lie Donald attempted to perpetuate.

Donald likely resented his father's exiling him to NYMA, and despite how enthusiastically he took to the military trappings of the school, it's clear that his enthusiasm and respect did not and does not extend to the military itself. Evading the draft in the Vietnam era doesn't on its own constitute contempt for the military. However, when Trump joked with Howard Stern that trying to avoid venereal disease in the 1990s was "my own personal Vietnam," he revealed his lack of respect for soldiers killed or wounded in that war. The proprietary, possessive tone he adapts toward the officers he refers to as "my generals" offers further evidence of his contempt for the armed forces, as do his attacks on Gold Star families. If Donald Trump's military school experience was supposed to instill in him a genuine respect for the military that extends beyond an affinity for its trappings, then in that respect it failed. For someone to emerge from an involuntary exile to military school with such disregard for the true principles of the military is certainly something that merited close examination before his being named commander-in-chief.

Another way Fred Trump's exiling Donald to NYMA failed is frighteningly evident in one of his most revealing remarks to D'Antonio. When reflecting on his behavior prior to his father's disruptive attempt to improve Donald's character with the enforced discipline of military school, Trump essentially admitted that the attempt was unsuccessful. "'I don't think people change very much,' Trump would tell me," D'Antonio reports. "'When I look at myself in the first grade and I look at myself now, I'm basically the same. The temperament is not that different.'" Such a bold proclamation of a presidential candidate's belief in the immutability of the personality should obviously have been cause for specific further inquiry. That it was coming from an individual who thinks he hasn't changed since the time when he was throwing rocks into the playpen of a neighboring toddler makes the remark all the more troubling. Worse still is the presence in his story of the significant intervening variable of involuntary military schooling. Intentionally or not, Trump is clearly signaling that his particular brand of aggression resists any effort to modulate it—a point that also merited consideration among supporters who bought into the fantasy that candidate Trump would pivot into a more presidential persona, and who continue to hold out hope that Trump has untapped wells of judgment and maturity that he will be able to access in a time of crisis.

Not surprisingly, Trump does contradict himself elsewhere when assessing his NYMA experience and the lessons it taught him. Reports D'Antonio, "When he reflected on this period, Trump would tell me, 'I was an elite person. When I graduated, I was a very elite person.'" Trump's progress along a teenager's vision of some absolute version of an "eliteness scale" offers little to assuage concerns about his frame of mind then or now.

In terms of learning the lesson that Fred perhaps most wanted to convey to his son, however, the banishment to NYMA accomplished its mission, establishing a power dynamic between father and son that lasted for the rest of Fred's lifetime and beyond. Sending Donald to NYMA may have constituted an admission by Fred that his son was uncontrollable, but it also sent Donald the message that if anyone was going to control him it was his father. Despite various challenges to his father's authority and/or primacy that we will explore in the next chapter, Donald made it startlingly clear in a 2016 interview with the *New York Times*'s Jason Horowitz who retained the upper hand; when asked what he thought his father would have thought about his run for president, Trump replied, "He would have absolutely allowed me to have done it." When crafting the "persona" of Donald Trump, bestselling author Trump wrote in *The Art of the Deal* that he "was never intimidated by my father, the way most people were. I stood up to him, and he respected that." The admission that running for president would have required his father's permission, of course, suggests otherwise.

How could Fred Trump have drawn the lines of authority so indelibly? Other than handing him a family business and untold resources with which to launch his own self-made myth, banishing Donald to NYMA was Fred's single most impactful assertion of his influence over Donald, but it wasn't the only lesson in obedience to which Donald could pay heed. To better understand Fred's hold on his second son, it's worth considering what happened to his first, Fred Jr.

Chapter Three

BROTHER

You can't have your brothers and eat them too.

—*Budd Schulberg,* What Makes Sammy Run?

Eight years Donald's senior, Fred and Mary's second-born child, Fred Jr., was groomed to inherit the family business from his father. It was never a good fit, however; described by the *New York Times*'s Jason Horowitz as "handsome, gregarious and self-destructive," Freddy Trump "lacked the killer instinct" that Fred Sr. sought to cultivate in his children. No match for his father's aggressive and demanding style, Freddy was unable to withstand his father's relentless criticism and abandoned the effort to follow in his father's professional footsteps. After a career as a pilot at Trans World Airlines, his life descended into alcoholism, which led to an early death at the age of forty-three, by which time, Horowitz writes, Freddy had "drifted so far from his father's ambitions that his children were largely cut out of the patriarch's will."

Freddy reportedly cautioned Donald about the dangers of alcoholism, but what he may have ultimately most vividly illustrated to his younger brother were the dangers of being a Trump.

In what is perhaps the most detailed account of the contentious failed attempt to pass the family-business baton from father to eldest son, Blair writes in *The Trumps*:

> When Freddy made what his father considered a mistake, such as installing new windows when old ones were still marginally serviceable, his father didn't hesitate to chew him out in public for wasting money; when Fred Jr. did something well, as when he finished off the roof and the final touches on a six-story Brooklyn building called the Falcon, his father never mentioned it. "When I asked him why not," Maryanne recalled, "he said, 'Why? He's supposed to do a good job.' It never occurred to him to actually praise Freddy."
>
> Tensions between father and son increased under the stress of the State Investigation Commission hearings on Trump Village, and they heightened further when Fred Jr. was unable to realize Fred Sr.'s hopes for Steeplechase Park. Freddy oversaw the dismantling of the old pavilion and stoutly defended his father's plans to the press, but he could not go forward when his father's political allies could not deliver the zoning variances needed for more high-rise apartment buildings.

Decades later, as Donald speaks in self-evaluating superlatives about the "greatest" and "best" people and results he gets, it's easy to see that he's not only compensating—he is praising himself because his father never praised anyone, doing for himself what his father never did for him or his ill-fated older brother.

The enmity between father and son predates the latter's ill-fated foray into the family business. Citing school-age friends of Fred Jr., Blair writes that Freddy's "obvious vulnerability" elicited a "harsh response" from his father, as observed by a contemporaneous friend. "Around us, his dad could be very aggressive, arrogant, and pushy, barely sociable in some ways," this friend told Blair. "He wanted tough people, that was his bottom line, and he put a lot of pressure on Freddy to achieve these goals." Fred Sr. was possibly projecting some of his own sibling rivalry onto the tension between his sons. Writes Blair: "When one of Freddy's crowd mentioned that he was going to study liberal arts at an Ivy League school, Fred Sr. bristled with rage and spoke contemptuously of how little money his own brother made as a full professor at MIT. 'I think Freddy's father feared that he would be an aesthete fairy, a little English gentleman,' said the friend. 'It was almost as though he thought prep school was emasculating his son, that he was having the aggressive instincts schooled out of him and he was being turned into an Ivy League wimp.'"

Freddy could well have been coming up against extant family dynamics made all the more powerful by predating him. Blair writes of Fred Sr.'s younger brother, John, an esteemed physicist, that "the MIT professor and his family were an intellectual crew, respected for their academic accomplishments but considered to have little practical sense. 'He had the brains,' Fred Trump once said gloatingly to a mutual acquaintance, 'but I made the money.'" Fred Sr.'s rivalry with his own brother can be seen as creating a model for a sibling rivalry that he projected onto and perhaps even cultivated in his sons. Because his definition of power was wealth and the ability to push other people around, Fred Sr. had contempt for his brother and what he perceived as his brother's weakness—a scenario he repeated with his first two sons—to the benefit of one and the tragic expense of the other.

The prospect of a sibling rivalry contributing to the premature death by alcoholism of the losing sibling is understandably a dynamic that a family might want to talk about. The eldest sibling, Maryanne, the only other family member to go on the record for Blair's account, downplayed the notion of competition between the brothers. "Donald moved ahead as Freddy failed," Maryanne said later. "I don't think there was a connection. Donald was a lot younger, not close enough in age for heavy competition. I don't think Freddy thought Donald was a cold wind at his back, and he wouldn't have cared if he was." Perhaps it doesn't matter whether Freddy cared, because Donald clearly did, telling Blair, "He was the first Trump boy out there, and I subconsciously watched his moves." Blair concludes that Donald "saw that cowering when his father got mad only made him angrier, that hanging around people who seemed more pointy headed than practical caused his father to fly into a rage, and that showing any vulnerability around his father was a mistake." Donald got the message: if he didn't want to spend his life behind the eight ball, he would have to show his father that he was every bit as tough as he was, that whenever anyone pushed him he would push right back and harder—that he was in spirit, if not in fact, first among the firstborns.

Contributing to the possibility of rivalry were some dynamics in play between the two brothers simply as a result of the order in which they were born. Second sons are often born into the position of having something to prove, especially when the elder brother is given the father's name. Donald knew that his older brother was named after their father, while Donald's name came from his mother's Scottish family, not his father's, and that nothing he could do would change that. Ultimately, despite becoming his father's functional heir, he experiences his place in the family as an imposter named Trump, because he isn't the eldest son.

Trump's unconscious fears of being exposed as an imposter can be seen as an ongoing, significant motivating force. The urgency of his attacks on Obama for being an imposter, for example, makes more sense when they are seen as projections of his own fears. Complicating Trump's fears of being labeled, or exposed, as an imposter is the simple fact that he has demonstrated he is fully and knowingly capable of being an imposter, by posing as other people, most notoriously the pseudonymous "John Barron," whose identity Donald would sometimes assume when talking to the press in the 1990s. That experiential knowledge of his capacity for illegitimacy haunts him to this day, particularly in regards to the charges of campaign collusion with Russia, which he either fears exposure of or knows his capacity for, or both. Regardless of Russia's participating, Trump will never get over losing the popular vote to Hillary Clinton any more than he got over being the second-born son.

Being the second son is not without advantages that Donald likely leveraged to his benefit. Blair quotes a camp counselor assessment that Freddy "wasn't as intelligent as Maryanne" and "wasn't quick enough to grasp what their father was telling him, which must have been hard given that he was the oldest boy." Though he was excoriated by his father for doing what would be objectively considered the right thing by anyone other than his father, Freddy's biggest shortcoming may have been that he simply didn't know how to read others—a capacity that many firstborn sons lack, deprived of the opportunities for social jockeying that younger siblings have, as they compete for attention and resources.

Whether Freddy lost the title of being heir apparent or Donald won it, the result had the appearance of a victory: in Blair's telling, "what could have been the biggest and most difficult conflict of [Donald's] entire career was over" before he finished high school, "and he had come out on top." Donald certainly had the chance to figure out how not to lose by watching what happened to his older brother. But there's enough ambiguity in his triumph that the story Donald tells himself of being the chosen one never satisfies; he has to continue to be chosen by more people than his father, which has ultimately led to his pursuit of being known and celebrated worldwide.

Does Donald feel at all complicit in Freddy's downfall? Trump assesses his older brother's plight very succinctly in *The Art of the Deal*: "Along the way, I think Freddy became discouraged, and he started to drink, and that led to a downward spiral. At the age of forty-three, he died. It's very sad, because he was a wonderful guy who never quite found himself. In many ways he had it all, but the pressures of our particular family were not for him. I only wish I had realized this sooner." With the generalization "our particular family," Trump almost confesses that he had a part in competitively pressuring his brother; clearly he's part of his "particular family," so he inevitably played some kind of role in Freddy's deterioration and defection from the other Trumps. He is also saying that, at a profound level, he was out of touch with his unconscious destructiveness when he says he wished he had realized this sooner. If he were aware of his own murderousness, perhaps he would have held himself back. How could he have not known how destructive he was, unless he projected his own competitiveness onto Freddy? Yet he appears to remain unaware of his destructiveness even as president, always blaming others for the consequences of his actions—never more clearly than in his insistence that the Democrats are responsible for the "death" of Deferred Action for Childhood Arrivals (DACA), a program that he ended. When he goes on the attack—usually by tweet—he justifies his aggression by claiming the other party started it. His need to dismantle, if not actually destroy, every regulation Obama imposed on business is what Trump perceives as a logical counterattack to his predecessor's having put destructive brakes on unfettered capitalism.

Elsewhere in that first memoir, Trump's version of the building-blocks story is tellingly laced with elements of passivity that appear to downplay his fraternal competitiveness (in this instance with his younger brother, Robert). "I wanted to build a very tall building, but it turned out that I didn't have enough blocks," he writes. "I asked Robert if I could borrow some of his, and he said, 'Okay, but you have to give them back when you're done.' I ended up using all of my blocks, and then all of his, and when I was done, I'd created a beautiful building. I liked it so much that I glued the whole thing together. And that was the end of Robert's blocks." In this presentation, in which it "turned out" that he lacked the blocks he wanted, and he "ended up" using all the blocks, Trump soft-pedals his agency in the story—at least up to the point where he has "created a beautiful building." Trump has been bragging about "beautiful" buildings, creations, and deals ever since—perhaps mindful of how many others' proverbial blocks have been appropriated in the process.

But elsewhere there is evidence that Donald joined his

father in belittling his big brother. Harry Hurt III writes that "Donald gave him unmitigated grief about his supposedly inferior station in life" after he quit the real estate business to become a TWA pilot. According to Hurt, Donald told Freddy, "There's no difference between what you do and driving a bus." That kind of sadistic insult is far from unfamiliar in Trump's current discourse, of course, but anyone with a conscience might regret such harsh judgments if their recipient subsequently lapsed into fatal alcoholism.

SIBLING RIVALRY IS THE oldest murder story in the Bible. Regardless of whether Donald is consciously haunted by guilt over his possible role in Freddy's destruction, he is almost certainly vulnerable to fear over Freddy's sad fate. To observe a brother suffer so profoundly likely gave young Donald more reason to fear his father, who initiated the abusive behavior toward Freddy. Donald's joining in his father's aggression can be seen as a vivid illustration of an unconscious attempt to protect himself by mirroring his father's characteristics. After all, if Fred Sr. could destroy Freddy, he could destroy Donald too. And the fear of such a consequential downfall could endure long beyond his father's death; decades later, battered by his own failures, Donald was compensating for the likely fears that what happened to Freddy could happen to him. By creating a grandiose defensive sense of omnipotence, Donald presented himself—at least to his father—as greater than he probably feared he was. To this day, he continues to do the same, as if the entire world symbolizes his father.

Some accounts of Freddy's downfall suggest that he voluntarily "turned away from Fred Sr." and the family business, as Hurt put it. Freddy's rebellion against his father was evident in college, where, according to David Cay Johnston, he claimed to be Jewish in order to join a Jewish fraternity—a passive-aggressive attack on his anti-Semitic father. Hurt suggests that Freddy's drive to follow his father to the head of the family empire was dampened by the eldest son's reaction to his father's history of scandal. "Donald had been only eight years old when his father was tarred by the 1954 scandal over windfall profits at the Shore Haven and Beach Haven projects," writes Hurt. "Freddy had been sixteen. He could not help feeling betrayed and embarrassed by the shame Fred Sr. had brought to the family name by being identified as one of the kingpins in the FHA affair. By the time he graduated from college, he was also aware of his father's hypocritical double life. The old man had recently transferred his religious affiliation to the Marble Collegiate Church in Manhattan, where he listened rapturously to Dr. Norman Vincent Peale's pop psychological preaching about *The Power of Positive Thinking*. But Fred Sr.'s reputation as the King of Miami Beach was no secret to his children." The family lore is that Freddy wasn't the "killer" that Fred raised Donald to be, but a disenchanted son could have simply decided that he was less willing to adopt his father's ways—skimming and taking advantage of others—that his younger brother was willing to have baked into his psyche.

Hurt's account may be the only example in print about the Trump children's disillusion with their father. It's not hard to imagine how devastating the sentiments could have been for Fred Jr., or how profoundly they challenge the "official" explanation for Freddy's failure, which blames the son's gentle nature more than the father's hostile disregard for business and social norms—a disregard that Donald had to embrace in order to succeed where his brother hadn't.

In retrospect Donald rewrites his past to say how much he honors his father—which contributes to the evidence that he actually feared his father. And a childhood fear of the father reverberates well into adulthood, undermining the adult's ability to think clearly and interactively. Thus Donald is rarely direct in his aggression toward others—tweeting his hostility while hiding inside a safe space.

Donald also rewrites his past to downplay the help he received from his family. Donald has repeatedly boasted of his Ivy League education and his Wharton pedigree, but he knows he owes that opportunity in part to his older brother. Blair writes that Fred Jr. had identified Wharton as "the top choice for Fred Sr.'s successor, but the older boy had been unable to gain admission. Heeding Freddy's example, Donald had not applied to Wharton straight off but had instead spent his senior year at NYMA, leafing through the dozens of college catalogs he kept in a little duffel bag under his desk. Now, after two years of respectable grades at Fordham and an interview with a friendly Wharton admissions officer who was one of Freddy's old high school classmates, Donald was able to transfer there."

In that instance it was Fred Jr. who came to Donald's rescue, but more frequently the rescuer was Fred Sr., who repeatedly helped Donald escape financial trouble, which Donald has also minimized in accounts of his rise to the top. Donald's reliance on his father's generosity offers a sharp point of contrast between him and his older brother. After Fred Jr.'s brief time in the family business, he pursued a career in aviation—a field in which he could distinguish himself with no evident assistance from his father's name or fortune. Donald, on the other hand, not only traded on his father's name and connections but relied on his financial support as well—from the almost certainly understated "small loan" of $1 million he has admitted to receiving from his father at the beginning of his real estate career to the millions of dollars in chips that Fred Sr. bought at one of Donald's casinos in a clever move that went around bankruptcy regulations that were barely keeping Donald afloat.

Despite witnessing his father's capacity to destroy Freddy, Donald on some unconscious level tended to rely on his father to rescue him. Over time he has shifted to simply expecting that rescue would materialize. Freddy, on the other hand, suffered and died beyond the reach of rescue; as anyone who has watched a loved one die of alcoholism can attest, the family's powerlessness over the progression of the disease is so devastatingly absolute as to make a mockery of the very idea of rescue.

Trump's irrational faith that somehow he would always be saved could well be a further manifestation of the trauma surrounding his brother's downfall; a deluded belief that everything is going to be okay, no matter what, could arise as a defense against recognizing that he shared either his brother's vulnerability or his father's aggression, or both. Yet looking at some of the dramatic reversals over his career, including his ascension to greater financial heights than ever after several of his businesses declared bankruptcy, one can see how Trump could come to believe that he would always indeed be rescued, whatever he did. In the final, wildly profitable years of his pre-political business career, his finances were restored by refocusing his businesses from construction and development to branding the Trump name—rescued once again by his father's name, if not by his father himself.

Further distancing himself from his brother and identifying with his father, Trump now assumes the role of the opposite of a person requiring rescue. Playing the part of the rescuer, Trump can now stand before an audience of political supporters searching for a savior and declare, "I alone can fix it." Trump's belief that he is the rescuing savior he portrays himself to be is no doubt fueled in part by his unconsciously knowing that he is not. He is neither his doomed brother, whose place in the family he once envied, nor his father, whose strength he both aspired to and feared. Their protracted deaths by alcoholism and Alzheimer's, respectively, demonstrated to Donald that no one is invincible. Now the family patriarch, Donald is unmoored, left only with his pathological coping mechanisms completely unchecked. He has to believe he is a savior because it would be too painful to admit that he isn't.

But the painful lessons of his brother's death no doubt color his memories of his father. Decades later, Kranish and Fisher asked then-candidate Trump about his older brother's misfortune, and the response might have sounded introspective to anyone unfamiliar with the oft-repeated family line: "'Freddy just wasn't a killer,' Donald said, echoing the term his father liked to use for a successful son." The implication, of course, is that someone else in the story *was* a killer, though Donald doesn't indicate whether the label applies to his father, himself, or both.

Donald also told Kranish and Fisher that Freddy's death was "the saddest part of what I've been through." The lesson he learned from his brother's experience, he confided, was "to keep my guard up one hundred percent," never acknowledging that the force who his brother failed to guard against was their own father. The feelings were even more unguarded in the immediate aftermath of Freddy's death, Kranish and Fisher report: "'Man is the most vicious of all animals, and life is a series of battles ending in victory or defeat,' Trump said two months after his brother's death. 'You just can't let people make a sucker out of you.'"

The story of Fred Jr.'s downfall is thus inextricably linked with the story of Donald's survival. Witnessing the tragic consequences of his brother being hounded out of the family business, Donald saw that the only way he could be protected from his father was to side with him at all costs. He was terrified of ending up like Freddy. The construct "If you can't beat 'em, join 'em" omits the likelihood that somebody else is going to get hurt. Candidate Trump's assumption of the role of the savior who will "make America great again" is the most extreme example of his identification with the aggressor: he takes on his father's mantle and aims not just to protect a wayward brother but to save an entire nation. But as a defense mechanism, identification with the aggressor is of only limited efficacy; instead of extinguishing the anger that the victim has for the abuser, this pattern of identification only obscures or redirects it. The unresolved hostility then exerts a powerful force, as the injury is passed along to other victims. In Trump's case, those victims may ultimately prove to include all who believe Trump will live up to his claims of coming to their rescue.

Chapter Four

RIVALS

If you do not get even, you are just a schmuck! . . .
I love getting even. I get screwed all the time. I go
after people, and you know what? People do not
play around with me as much as they do with
others. They know that if they do, they are in for
a big fight. Always get even.

> —*Donald J. Trump,* Think Big and
> Kick Ass in Public Life

I t is fitting that before he entered politics, Donald Trump
acquired his highest level of fame not as a builder, a deal
maker, a negotiator, or a tycoon, but as a TV character on a reality competition show. More than anything, Donald Trump is
a competitor. Donald Trump has been competing his whole
life—as a brother, as an athlete, as a businessman, as a reality
television personality, and now as a politician. He has profited—
or would have profited, if he had been a better businessman—
off the universal competitive instinct that he attempted to

leverage in his casinos, football team, and beauty pageants. But the competition that most shaped Donald's psyche has been as a son; Donald's competition with his father has had more impact on the development of his personality than any other competition, and continues to reverberate now on a global scale, years after his father's death.

Trump writes in *The Art of the Deal* that he "didn't want to be in the business my father was in," the business he describes as "building rent-controlled and rent-stabilized housing in Queens and Brooklyn . . . a very tough way to make a buck." Trump writes that he "wanted to try something grander, more glamorous, and more exciting." At the outset, he clearly wanted to outperform his father at least on the glamour and excitement scales. Implicit in his characterization of his father's business, however, was Donald's rejection of the rules and regulations that burned his father and narrowed the lane in which landlords seeking their fortunes in the rent-controlled and rent-stabilized markets could maneuver. He is still revisiting his competition with his weaker, rule-bound father when he rolls back rules and regulations as president.

Elsewhere in *The Art of the Deal*, he contrasts the aspirational elements of his and his father's approaches. "My father built low-income and middle-income buildings in Brooklyn and Queens, but even then, I gravitated to the best location," he writes. "When I was working in Queens, I always wanted Forest Hills. And as I grew older, and perhaps wiser, I realized that Forest Hills was great, but Forest Hills isn't Fifth

Avenue." (This was, of course, decades before Donald came to refer to Fifth Avenue as the place where he could shoot someone without recourse.) "And so I began to look toward Manhattan, because at a very early age, I had a true sense of what I wanted to do. I wasn't satisfied just to earn a good living. I was looking to make a statement. I was out to build something monumental." This was written with the benefit of hindsight, of course, and there's nothing in the historical record that indicates young Donny Trump was indeed thinking at an early age about building anything monumental in Manhattan. We do know that he was going into Manhattan on surreptitious trips to make acquisitions for his knife collection. Manhattan was thus constructed in his adolescent mind as a place to challenge his father's authority, another form of competition with his father. Those trips underscore the delinquent core of Donny's character—his repetitive secret acts of defiance.

Before Donald got started in business, he accompanied his father to the dedication ceremony for the Verrazano-Narrows Bridge in November 1964. The bridge connects two of New York City's outer boroughs, Brooklyn and Staten Island, so it's somewhat surprising that Trump even acknowledges his attendance, but in fact he has turned the events into an often-repeated story in his narrative of his life.

"Amid the pageantry," goes the version in *Trump Revealed*, "Donald noticed that city officials barely acknowledged the bridge's eighty-five-year-old designer, Othmar Ammann. Although the day had been sunny and cloudless, Trump would remember pouring rain years later when he recalled Ammann's standing off to the side, alone. 'Nobody even mentioned his name,' Trump said. 'I realized then and there that if you let people treat you how they want, you'll be made a fool. I realized then and there something I would never forget: I don't want to be made anybody's sucker.'"

Trump's first biographer, Jerome Tuccille (*Trump: The Saga of America's Most Powerful Real Estate Baron*), wrote, "Donald must have made a conscious decision that day in 1964 to make sure his name was prominently stamped on everything he built. No one would ever forget his name at a dedication ceremony." As frightening as it may be to consider that the nation is being governed according to a conclusion reached by an eighteen-year-old—who claims his psychological development had stopped ten years prior—perhaps equally troubling is the degree to which the known facts are so liberally altered to fit Donald's narrative. The news photograph of the day shows clearly that the sun is shining, confirmed by the *New York Times* reporting on the event. The *Times* reports that the master of ceremonies did in fact forget to mention Ammann by name, but only after praising him as "the greatest living bridge engineer, perhaps the greatest of all time."

If anyone was overlooked that day it was Donald—the kid from Queens standing next to his father, barely visible in the news photograph, although appearing to try to be noticed. Donald's competitive impulses may well have been jolted into a higher gear that day, but as his fact-challenged re-creation of the story indicates, his mastery of what was actually going on is somewhat limited. But it was psychically less threatening for him to project the slight onto someone else rather than acknowledge the rivalry with the powerful and frightening father who from his perspective was making a fool of his elder brother, and whose characteristics he was already beginning to assume in his own defense to avoid his brother's fate.

When Donald did make the purportedly long-dreamed-about move into Manhattan real estate, it was over his father's objections—although it was very much consistent with Fred's model of profiting off others' misfortunes. The 1970 failure of the Penn Central Railroad was at the time the largest corporate bankruptcy in US history. Donald was interested in three of the Manhattan holdings that the railroad was forced to sell off— two large pieces of West Side real estate and the Commodore Hotel next to Grand Central Terminal. "Buying the Commodore at a time when even the Chrysler Building is in receivership is like fighting for a seat on the *Titanic*," Fred told Donald. But Donald persisted—backed by his father's equity, loan co-signs, and political connections—and turned the failed hotel into the Grand Hyatt.

As his *Art of the Deal* description of the protracted negotiations that led to his first big success makes clear, one of Donald's driving motivations was proving himself to his father. "But as the months went by," he writes, "the deal became more and more complicated and difficult . . . and the stakes rose for reasons unrelated to money. I could talk big for only so long. Eventually I had to prove—to the real estate community, to the press, to my father—that I could deliver the goods." Without his father around to prove his value to, Trump has had much more difficulty recognizing when he can no longer "talk big" without delivering the goods.

A few years later, one of the West Side real estate parcels that Donald had optioned from Penn Central—the Thirty-Fourth Street rail yards—was chosen by the city as the site for its new convention center. "Trump argued that his option on the property entitled him to a commission of more than $4 million," write Kranish and Fisher. "But he offered to waive the fee if the city named the facility the Fred C. Trump Convention Center." What appears at first blush to be a warm gesture of respect to his father looks somewhat hollow, however, when the full details are considered. A city official "revisited Trump's contract with Penn Central," Kranish and Fisher report, "and saw that his option actually entitled him to barely a tenth of the commission he was claiming." Donald was trying to sell his father's name for something he didn't in fact own. (Fred might have approved nonetheless.)

At the time of his biggest business achievement, the building of Trump Tower, Trump was canny enough to see how a father-son rift could create an opening for an opportunist such as himself to exploit. Trump was able to acquire the prime Manhattan land parcel on which the Bonwit Teller department store stood only because of a falling-out between the father and son in the company that controlled the department store. "Since I am so close to my father," Trump writes in *The Art of the Deal*, "I found the whole thing hard to believe, but the bottom line was that [the son] Franklin finally managed to push his father out and take over. And so, in 1975, it was Franklin I called to discuss my interest in Bonwit."

Donald's 1980s move into Atlantic City—which Oedipal-minded observers would point out was where his parents honeymooned, and thus in some respects the ultimate proving ground for a rival son to compete with his father—included strategies that he knew would earn his father's disapproval. Donald was already a partner in Harrah's at Trump Plaza (which later became simply Trump Plaza) when the Hilton Hotels Corporation, nearing completion of its own Atlantic City hotel and casino, was unexpectedly denied a New Jersey gaming license. Hilton sold Trump the hotel that would become Trump's Castle, in a deal that Trump describes in *The Art of the Deal* as being "almost entirely on my gut. I made my bid without ever walking through the hotel. . . . If I'd told my father the story, he would have said I'd lost my mind."

Trump's description of the deal is notable because of the attention it gives to yet another breakdown of the father-and-son relationship, this one leaving the Hilton family in a vulnerable position. "When Conrad died in 1979, he totally screwed Barron," Trump writes. "There is no nicer way to say it. The assumption had been that Conrad would pass on his near-controlling interest in the company to Barron—or at the very least that he'd spread it among family members. Instead, Conrad Hilton used his will to disenfranchise his children and grandchildren." Trump continues, "Conrad believed very strongly that inherited wealth destroys moral character and motivation," a position with which Trump himself "happen[s] to agree that it often does." Trump then observes that Conrad left Barron only "a token number of shares of stock, and he left each of his grandchildren a piddling $10,000 each," and characterizes Barron's ascension to the head of the company as having had "nothing to do with merit; it's called birthright." Elsewhere he dismisses Barron as a "member of what I call the Lucky Sperm Club" because so many of his advantages were bestowed on him only by birth. "He was born wealthy and bred to be an aristocrat, and he is one of those guys who never had to prove anything to anyone."

Perhaps Trump was already losing sight of the lucky circumstances of his own birth, or trying to score a victory against his father by denying the necessary assistance he provided to launch Donald's career. Of course, in an actual aristocracy the family castle goes to the firstborn son, and can't be bought and declared by the second son, so Trump's claiming acquisition of what he would rename as his family's castle represents a victory over both the Hilton family he considered dysfunctional and his own family. The fact that Trump bought it under terms that he knew his father would disapprove further highlights the unconscious aggression toward his father that motivated the purchase. But when, years later, Trump gave his third son the same aristocratic name as the "Lucky Sperm Club" member whom he bested by defying his own father's values, he added an element to the rivalry with Barron Hilton that makes the head spin.

By the mid-1980s, Trump was enough of a success celebrity that his breakthrough book, *Trump: The Art of the Deal*, included an eleven-step success formula. Step one, "Think Big," is an explicit statement of phallic narcissism. Its roots go back to early childhood, with the son effectively saying, *Look how big I am, Daddy. My penis is bigger than yours.* In pictures of adult Donald with his father, we see the son towering over the man who once terrified the Trump household. The childhood fixation on size has continued into his political-career put-downs; the nicknames disparaging various foes as little (or "liddle") may overtly be about stature, but they are covertly about penis size as well.

If the president's penis seems like an uncomfortable or even humorous topic of discussion, remember that the president himself brought it up—on national television, during a presidential debate. Parents know that many a young boy makes his penis a focal point during the phallic narcissism phase, when he is prone to convey that his penis is the world's biggest and strongest, and worthy of admiration. This phase is particularly pronounced in boys with overactive fantasies of grandiosity, though most go through it in one way or another. A boy who fears shame or humiliation, however, may be less likely to develop the mature perspective that shifts focus away from the centrality of his penis. Instead, he may grow into an adult who emphasizes—often inaccurately—the superior size of his measurable accomplishments, from his fortune to his victories to his inauguration day audience. Or he may find means to compensate for his fear of humiliation—or, perhaps, for his being shamed by the inattentiveness of his parents, or for witnessing the shaming of a brother—by projecting his phallic narcissism outward to assert his triumph over his feared or shaming father.

Trump's phallic narcissism has been projected onto structures he's erected around the world. His towers dwarf his father's accomplishments while claiming—if not appropriating—the name they share. Drawing upon the way psychoanalysts have organized our understanding of the mental development of boys, it's safe to surmise that Trump's rivalry with his father, as with every son and father, has something to do with the penis—its relative size, power, potency, and symbolic implication. The reverse is also true: Donald Trump's relationship to his penis, so vividly on display in skylines around the world, has something to do with his rivalry with his father.

Freud labeled the archetypal father-son rivalry as the Oedipus complex, which ultimately involves the boy's desire to kill his father and claim his mother. What the boy experiences as fear of the father's wrath is in fact a defense against recognizing his own aggression projected onto his father. When a boy is able to re-own his aggression, he may feel the need to repair any damage he might have done. But with a boy like young Donald, whose early development impeded any ability to recognize and then modify his likely patricidal fantasies, the aggression remains unchecked. In these boys the aggressive impulse toward the father can be redirected and expanded into a general destructive impulse that can continue long past childhood.

In addition to fearing Fred's retaliation, Donald also fears feelings of shame because he still needs his father, so he transforms those fears into destructive hostility that he directs elsewhere—often at the weak and needy, who remind him unconsciously of his own unacceptable needs. Driven to emulate and outperform the father he unconsciously holds responsible for his humiliation—past and future—he is highly motivated to direct his destructive impulses on symbolic reminders of his father's strength and his own weakness.

While the Oedipal perspective on adult phallic narcissism suggests that a son exhibiting such behavior is seeking to defeat his father by exhibiting his superior strength, a man like Donald Trump seeks his father's approval as much as his defeat. The son of a tyrannical father, threatened by witnessing the crushing discipline inflicted on his brother, yearns for the father's love as protection against father's potential wrath. What's more, given the need to defend his fragile sense of self, this yearning raises strong feelings of vulnerability, giving added impetus to erecting a false macho self. He also has to defend people who remind him of his father, like the white supremacists marching in Charlottesville.

As president, Trump is driven to continue his pursuit of exciting triumphs, a repetition compulsion that never allows him to find an emotional resting place. He needs the excitement of a looming paternal threat as well; no longer dominated by the simple drive to outperform, he needs more dangerous menace and flirtation with potential ruin, and the excitement of experiencing how frightened he becomes. At the same time, he is compelled to try to discredit and defeat the father figure that menaces him. We see this in full flower in Trump's obsession with Robert Mueller, the FBI, and the Russia probe. Clearly Trump knows that his campaign engaged in at least some questionable contact with the Russians, if not outright collusion, and he has taken at least some steps to discourage, if not outright obstruct, this discovery. His attempts to avoid being caught are a replay of his delinquent adolescent treks into Manhattan to buy switchblades. Trump's terror of this investigation is also a dramatic replay of his fear of his father, with Mueller a vivid reminder of how suddenly he can be removed and exiled, as when his father banished him to NYMA. By attacking Mueller's integrity and trying to break his resolve, he is attempting both to protect himself from exile and get even with his father for rejecting him.

For decades, Donald Trump has been attempting to avoid being unmasked by his father, developing an arsenal of protective defenses—combativeness, bullying, impulsivity, and an authoritarian attitude, all the while appearing to imitate Fred Sr. But overtly, he felt he was unique. Despite claiming self-reliance, Donald's business record reveals that his father was a frequent source of direct and indirect support, from early political and industry connections to financial assistance to the incalculable value of the Trump family name. Though Donald obviously depended on such help, he was unable to muster any sense of gratitude, impeded by his envy of his father's power, and the enduring wound of rejection. This inability to acknowledge the assistance on which he depended contributed in Donald to a chronic state of dissociation.

The dissociated individual, divorced from his emotions, often manifests cruelty and duplicity without any apparent self-awareness or remorse. These attributes of Trump's pathology will merit further exploration in subsequent chapters. Dissociation profoundly limits the capacity to feel empathy, as the individual who is emotionally disconnected from his own suffering will predictably not recognize it in others. Donald Trump's lifelong defense of protecting himself through his well-constructed bravado may appear successful, but unconsciously he is recreating the painful indifference that he felt from his parents. Protectively dissociated from his own discomfort, he lacks the psychic resources to feel compassion for the suffering of others, let alone express it.

Dissociation, however, doesn't accomplish the affected individual's goal of getting rid of his unwanted feelings, and is often accompanied by another only partially successful psychic defensive strategy—the predictable cycle of projection and attack. Trump unconsciously avoids the frightening prospect of experiencing the shame he feels about his dependency on his critical father by projecting his unwanted vulnerability onto others, then attacking them for being weak. Admitting his dependency is so potentially painful and humiliating to him that he has even engaged in public disparagement of his own father's power, as when he expressed contempt for the "Lucky Sperm Club" and implied that he wasn't himself a member.

The implication that his father's sperm isn't lucky—and thus, presumably, inferior to his own—again brings to mind the thinking of the young phallic narcissist, who perceives his penis as the source of his power. When this primitive understanding is projected onto the father, the boy may confuse his longing for paternal love and power with a sexual desire for his father's penis. As speculative as this interpretation may seem, the individual who unconsciously creates this false equivalency may react with alarm, soon followed by a cycle of projection and attack. In this scenario, the individual projects his misunderstood longing onto homosexual men, whom he unconsciously views as contemptible reflections of disavowed parts of himself. He then seeks to expel his contempt for these unwanted impulses by attacking those who openly express them, which Trump's record on LGBT issues indicates he is all too willing to do.

As if to overcompensate for those unwanted feelings, Donald aggressively asserted his pursuit of a path different from his father's when it came to women. While Fred was said to have a reputation as a womanizer, he kept any dalliances out of the eyes of the public—and his family—and remained married to his first and only wife until his death. Donald, on the other hand, has been famously public about his escapades, facilitating and cultivating press coverage of his personal life that peaked with the front-page tabloid treatment of the affair with Marla Maples that ended his marriage to his first wife, Ivana.

Fred Trump, as competitive as his son, reportedly saw their respective family and personal lives as yet another field of competition. And while some may see the son as at least trying to outperform his father by having so many public affairs and marital dramas, Fred saw his son's public restlessness as making him the loser in that particular competition. "[Donald] Trump ultimately eclipsed his father," wrote the *New York Times* in 2016, "though Fred Trump, who was married to his wife for more than 60 years, joked to his thrice-married son that the 'one place you'll never beat me is with the marriage stuff.'"

It's unclear, however, whether Fred declared himself the victor because he stayed married or because he was simply never caught cheating. Hurt writes of a conversation between father and son after Donald's flouting of his marital vows to Ivana attracted some "unwelcome scrutiny" from the Division of Gaming Enforcement. "In his own heyday the elder Trump's alleged extramarital dalliances along the Florida Gold Coast had earned him a reputation as the 'King of Miami Beach,'" writes Hurt. But Fred was "furious at Donald" for his extramarital behavior jeopardizing his professional standard. Hurt continues: "'You can have a thousand mistresses if you want,' Fred Trump lectured his son, 'but you don't have just one. And whatever you do, you never, ever let yourself get caught.'" Fred was so angry that the still-married Donald invited Marla to the opening of the Trump Taj Mahal that he said he would not attend if she came. Donald disinvited her, giving lie to his claim that he always stood up to his father.

In some respects Donald's competition with his father still continues today—for example, in the time and energy he spends every morning to assemble his trademark of improbably colored and positioned hair. While Fred Trump was no stranger to hair dye either, photographs indicate he did nothing to hide his dramatically receding hairline. Donald, on the other hand, "had a tremendous fear of baldness," according to former Trump casino executive and biographer John O'Donnell. "He once observed to [fellow casino executive Mark Eless] that he considered baldness a sign of weakness . . . warning him, 'The worst thing a man can do is go bald. Never let yourself go bald.'" Trump tries to show the world he is stronger than his father with every careful comb-over—an illusion he will clearly go to great lengths to maintain.

In Fred's final years, Donald witnessed his father fall prey to the ravages of time, as his slow decline from Alzheimer's gradually incapacitated him. Trump no doubt felt the loss of that competition in his father's wake. The day of Fred's burial was "by far the toughest day of my life," he told Kranish and Fisher, adding that "he felt 'loneliness and responsibility, because I was really close to my father.' He began to see himself differently, not just as the new family patriarch or as a builder, but as someone who could help shape the world. . . . Years later, Trump would say his father's death was perhaps what 'inwardly' pushed him to finally decide he wanted to be president. The decision had been years in the making."

If the loss of his father spurred Trump to pursue his biggest competition yet—his pursuit of the presidency—it likely also sparked a resurgence in his father hunger as well. Deprived of paternal empathy as a child, Trump still yearns for a father, an unconscious desire expressed in his attraction to Steve Bannon, Michael Cohen, and even the much younger—but more overtly confident—French President Emmanuel Macron. Unable to express those needs directly, he instead acts as the grandiose or occasionally affectionate leader who, for example, picks a piece of dandruff off Macron's coat. This presentation of self is part of a compensatory narcissism, dramatized perhaps most memorably at the Republican National Convention, when his arrival on the stage was preceded by a giant shadow emerging from fog.

The yearning for a father is also evident in his pathological search for authority in the kinds of leaders to whom he is drawn—Rodrigo Duterte, Recep Tayyip Erdogan, Xi Jinping, and most notably Vladimir Putin. Unfortunately, none of those father figures appears to stimulate a competitive response from Trump. Instead, Trump's lifelong search for a male authority figure who values and admires him in a way that resembles a dynamic that was missing from the father-son relationship has led him to seem almost spellbound by Macron's flattery, after a place of cooperation with adversaries with whom the responsibilities of his office would appear to require him to compete. As we'll see in the chapters ahead, the pathology that emerged from Trump's early years and formative relationships is characterized by a number of essential elements that would be of particular interest to any adversary looking to predict his level of cooperativeness based on his psychological profile.

PART TWO

PATHOLOGIES

Chapter Five

THE PSYCHOLOGY
OF LYING

No man has a good enough memory to be a successful liar.

⁀Abraham Lincoln

Lying is universal—we all do it; we all must do it.

⁀Mark Twain

E veryone knows that President Trump lies; even his legal team maneuvered in early 2018 to keep him out of circumstances where he would have to testify under oath for fear that any situation requiring him to curtail his uncertain narrative would constitute a "perjury trap." Trump himself has long acknowledged the lies on which he built his earliest career successes. Kranish and Fisher report that his first big success, the Penn Central deal to buy the Commodore Hotel, was concluded only through "a feat of misdirection he would later boast about" involving his supplying city officials with "what looked like an agreement with the sellers" in order to close the deal that the paperwork suggested was already closed. His partners in his first Atlantic City casino project, he writes in *The Art of the Deal*, came on board after he staged a construction-site scene that would "assure them that my casino was practically finished," when "in reality, I wasn't that far along"—a sleight of hand that he characterized as "confirming an impression they were already predisposed to believe." During his bankruptcies a few years later, Kranish and Fisher write, "Trump clung to his billionaire image. 'It's ridiculous,' he said of suggestions that he lacked the cash to pay contractors who had built the Taj. 'I have a lot of money.' Behind the scenes, however, Trump was frantically negotiating with his bankers."

Trump's habitual, strategic, and vocal departures from the factual record have been so prevalent in his approach to business and life that he coined a phrase for the practice: "truthful hyperbole," an appropriately oxymoronic phrase for a practice that unconsciously conveys contempt for language, meaning, and trust. More recently, his presidential enabling squad put forth yet another equally meaningless attempt to make lying more palatable, the infamous Kellyanne Conway theory of "alternative fact." His lies have become so commonplace that a cottage industry of non-alternative-fact checkers has emerged in the mainstream media, calling unprecedented attention to the president's apparently uncontrollable reliance on the lie as a basic building block of his communication strategy. The

Washington Post, for example, tallied over two thousand "false or misleading claims" during Trump's first year in office.

Everybody lies, which is a blessing and a curse when trying to assess the deeper dimensions of the pathology of Donald Trump's lying, and the grave threat to the nation that it represents. Most of us don't want to consider the possibility that the lies we tell might place the lives and well-being of everyone around us at risk. But most of us aren't courting catastrophe for ourselves and others with the often-little lies we tell, because most of us aren't pathological liars. And most of us, of course, haven't deliberately expanded the impact of the lies we tell by falsely soliciting and winning the trust of millions.

Because there's at least a little bit of a liar in so many of us, it is easy for most of us to underestimate the risk of awarding the nation's highest office to an individual whose psychological profile so closely hews to the definition of pathological liar. Now America has taken that risk and elected a president driven by specific psychic impulses far beyond what the casual liar might identify with. The pathological liar is driven by unconscious factors so powerful as to make it almost impossible not to lie. To the pathological liar, lying is an addiction and a perversion that unconsciously serves as a source of protection and power—defending against fears of rejection, blame, or loss while instilling a false sense of potency, control, and ability to manipulate others. Because most of us lie at times, we may be inclined to give a pathological liar the benefit of the doubt, but to do so is a mistake; the pathological liar is psychologically damaged, compelled by specific unconscious forces that are so powerful he cannot be trusted.

To most of us, lying simply involves not telling the truth—fabricating stories or falsifying facts in order to mislead others. We often associate it with criminals and con artists who deny wrongdoing to protect themselves or who manipulate others' perceptions for their benefit. Psychoanalytically, we speak of both lying to others and lying to oneself. They can both be done at the same time, of course, but ultimately the psychodynamic that drives lying to another is driven by the unconscious impulse to lie to oneself—to deny an aspect of reality that one doesn't want to face or accept.

The lie may have the consciously desired effect—of shielding the individual from the reality he wants to deny—but not without a cost. Psychoanalytically, lying emerges from the child's need to separate from the mother; just as the lie is a turn away from the truth, the childhood lie is an attempt to turn away from the mother. As we have seen elsewhere, the child's feelings toward the mother are a conflicted combination of need and resentment, a dynamic that typically serves as the first source of anxiety in a child. The lie is an attempt to manage that anxiety, by asserting agency and independence from the mother.

The first time the child's lie is believed, he achieves a level of separation from the mother heretofore unexperienced. The experience is freeing; the child feels separate, private, and in control. But it is also frightening, because he has separated himself from the nurturing mother as well as the frustrating and withholding mother. The lie gets the child the desired goal—independence, if even for a moment—but it leaves him isolated and alone. The child's assertion of power has thus left him in a vulnerable state, and his response to that vulnerability is a powerful force in shaping his character. For some, the response is to assert power again, by telling another lie, and out of this sequence the pattern of habitual, even pathological, lying is sometimes born.

Psychoanalytic investigation of pathological lying often reveals that the pathological liar experienced some version of unreliable parenting. Biographers and observers note that Donald Trump often behaves like both his parents. His father was always working, and was present and available for his children only when they would visit him at work or at construction sites—a pattern Donald adapted to his own style of fathering by limiting his time spent with his children to workplace visits. His mother was largely absent for a different set of reasons, by multiple accounts more invested in the trappings of being a wealthy real estate developer's wife than in participating in the work of raising their children. Such circumstances beg the question of whether Donny felt that his parents lied to him, or couldn't be trusted to tell the truth. To a child who longed for attention, such parents must have seemed different from how they overtly behaved, professing love while often being absent or preoccupied.

If a child gets mixed messages from his parents, he may have trouble understanding which messages are genuine and which are false. It's easy to see how a child who felt that his parents loved the idea of having a son more than the fact of the son they had could grow into an adult who loves the idea of the image he projects more than the hard work of becoming and maintaining the reality the image suggests—who would love the idea of being president, for example, more than the fact of all the work his job entails. My forty years of clinical practice lead me to the conclusion that baby Donny's parents were likely the first people to deliver him "fake news."

As the pathological liar grows into adulthood, the sources of anxiety change, but the need to manage anxiety never goes away, and usually gets more pronounced. Each lie's small alteration of the truth represents the intention of making an even greater alteration to the truth; as they accrue, an entire system of misinformation emerges. Before he knows it, the liar is pressed into a new system defined by those alterations. That system becomes the new truth, and the liar can manage his anxiety only by maintaining the entire false system of lies; facts must be not what they are but what the compulsive system requires. Over time, he allows the new system of altered facts to be imposed on him, sustaining his need for certainty, which he requires in order to manage the original anxiety that drove him to lie in the first place.

Donald Trump's political career is built upon a lie—the

infamous "birther" lie with which he challenged Barack Obama's legitimacy. Like many of his lies, the content of Trump's false claim that Obama was born in Kenya resonates in ways worth exploring—the implicit racist fear of the "other," the projected fears of his own illegitimacy rooted in some level of self-knowledge about his failures as a businessman— but the unconscious impulse to lie preceded its actual formation. The simple fact of telling the outrageous lie that Obama was not a US citizen—and thus not the legitimate president— accomplished the same psychological goal as the first lie he told his mother: it asserted his independence, setting him apart from the other Obama critics and would-be candidates, in much the same way as lying little Donny likely set himself apart from his four siblings in the crowded Trump household decades ago. While Donny was a legitimate child, he wasn't a necessary one, because he already had an older brother named for their father. And no matter how much his father loved him, Donny would never be Fred Trump Jr.—his father's legitimate namesake.

Once the birther lie was told, Trump had set into motion the construction of a system built upon the foundational falsehood of Obama's illegitimacy. Thus the first lie begat equally dishonest subsequent expansions and elaborations—from claims of Trump's detectives corroborating the story abroad, even up to accusations that the illegitimate president unlawfully wiretapped the upstart candidate—as the system grew in tandem with Trump's need to make others believe in its false claims.

Observers often note with surprise how regularly Trump doubles down on the lies he tells, but the surprise is misplaced, because the unconscious purpose they serve prohibits him from doing anything else.

As the fictitious system grows, so does the opportunity for it to satisfy the liar's need for the anxiety-easing illusion of certainty. Thus we see Trump growing more certain after he is caught in a lie, as with the Trump Tower wiretapping accusation. The pathological liar likes to feel that he knows the truth—an illusion in which he is too invested to back down. He must cling to his lies to retain the necessary illusion of omniscience, which would be jeopardized by any gesture of correction or apology. The affect of certainty has the added bonus of defensively discouraging the doubts of the others, whose belief in the fictional system the liar also needs.

Trump grew up in a fictional system that he continues unconsciously to mimic as president. In his first State of the Union speech, Trump told Puerto Rico, "We are with you; we love you; and we will pull through together." FEMA had already announced that food and water shipments would end the next day. With those false reassurances, President Trump re-created the dynamic of a distant mother professing love when she already knew she was about to withdraw it. He perfected the illusion of operating within a fictional system when he portrayed a successful businessman on reality television during a period of professional decline, performing on imaginary workplace sets constructed in Trump Tower to represent the far less impressive or industrious offices upstairs. And if Michael Wolff's central assertion is to be believed, Trump expanded his fictional system to its largest scale ever by running a presidential campaign he had no honest intention of winning. Now Trump goes through the motions of being president without ever being truly presidential. This now-familiar way of dealing with the public—saying one thing and meaning or doing something very different—is almost predictable when seen as an indication of experiences from his own past.

Some observers have speculated that the 2016 Trump campaign started, at least in the candidate's psyche, on the night of the 2011 White House Correspondents Association annual dinner, when Trump was relentlessly and effectively mocked from the dais—by host Seth Meyers and especially by President Obama, whose remarks zeroed in on Trump's propagation of the birther lie. For an individual consumed with appearances, the public roasting was no doubt humiliating. But the remarks' focus on the birther lies ultimately targeted not just Trump but the elaborate fictional system that he had to maintain in his mind—and in the minds of others—for it to serve the anxiety-management function for which it was unconsciously designed. The psychological stakes for Trump were higher than the delighted audience likely ever realized.

Whatever his conscious motives for initiating the birther-lie attack, his goal was never his own public humiliation. Psychoanalytic theory suggests that the child's first lie to his mother is an unconscious response to the resentment that stems from the first time he feels duped or humiliated by his mother—for turning her attention elsewhere. Powerful indeed are the circumstances in adulthood that evoke the deep-seated memories of that infant humiliation, especially for an individual who has been as public as Trump in his fear of and aversion to being humiliated or—as he put it in the life lesson he derived from witnessing the public neglect of the Verrazano-Narrows Bridge architect—"a sucker." When Trump was publicly humiliated for his birther lies—which were themselves rooted in memories of a long-ago humiliation—it was predictable, if not inevitable, that he would respond by clinging ever more ferociously and vociferously to the fictional system he created around Obama.

The childhood wound of feeling duped by his mother is never far from the surface with Trump. It enables him unconsciously to connect with his strongest supporters, whose own feelings of being wounded and misled perpetuate the system of lies he has constructed. A large percentage of his supporters had already indicated that they felt lied to, not only by DC politicians but also by the very mainstream media elites that humiliated Trump in 2011. That dynamic paradoxically facilitated Trump's lying to them at his rallies early in 2015. While his campaign lies had the overt appearance of being intended to help his audiences feel less betrayed, covertly they represented an unconscious attempt to gain power. As he evacuated into his audience his own feelings of having been duped, they become his fools the way he was once his mother's fool. But they are not his victims; his base already felt betrayed for years by detached Washington politicians, as they may have originally felt disappointed by their own parents years earlier. Trump instinctively recognizes their narcissistic wounds and gives them permission—even urges them—to vent their rage at having been ignored for so long.

In the heat of a campaign rally, however, when Trump is telling his audience the lies they want to hear, they feel like anything but fools. The pathological liar is driven by a need to re-create the feeling of infantile omnipotence—no longer by getting his mother to believe his lies but by convincing others to accept them. Why would they believe his lies? Because those who are gulled by the habitual liar have an unconscious need to share vicariously in the liar's omnipotence. In this way, Trump's outrageous lies have so much influence over his supporters not in spite of their outrageousness but because of it; Trump presents a dynamic that is unconsciously familiar to his base, who crave the illusion of omnipotence that he aspires to re-create with his lies and share vicariously in the sense of power he asserts, even as he tells lies that are ultimately at their own expense.

This works because there is a shared worldview—of a dangerous world where everyone is lied to and most likely everyone is lying as well. The ability to get away with lying in such a world is thus a source of comfort, a reflection of that shared worldview, and an assertion of power in an unsafe world.

We know enough about Trump's childhood to identify

reasons why he might have felt deceived as a child; the toddler whose mother is less available after the difficult birth of a younger sibling leaves her sickly and overwhelmed, can feel duped by what he experiences as the loss of her love and attention—just as the teenager can feel betrayed by the father who instills in him a belief that he is a king and a killer, only to be banished from home to the loveless confinement of military school. When an adult has processed his childhood experiences in this way, he carries into adulthood a childhood wound that has not healed, but from which some relief can at least be approximated by becoming the person who tricks others. In the case of Trump, his perhaps unconscious ability to identify and induce identification with like-minded individuals facilitates a powerful bond with his followers—who already feel duped and angry about more recent betrayals, and are thus easy marks for his lies.

Thus reversing the damaging dynamic of his own past, Trump unconsciously assumes the role of the parent who is now in the position to dupe the child—represented in his case by his followers, a broad swath of whom are at once suspicious of other, previous authority figures who have disappointed or deceived them in the past and are willing to suspend disbelief to be deceived by the unreliable Trump. On one level, Trump is unconsciously able to act as if he is the loving parent, denying to himself that his own parents ever disappointed him. But on another level he behaves exactly like his disappointing parents, treating even his base the way he once felt treated—with duplicity.

Sometimes the wounds of perceived childhood rejection are so profound that the child never feels loved at home and grows up unable to tell whether his true self can be accepted or loved. Trump's adult behavior is consistent with that pathology, with the lie implicit in his posture of omnipotence also serving as protection against the risk of showing how he felt inside. He can never feel loved, as seen by his relentless demands for reassurance from his cabinet members and whoever else might be recruited to regularly praise and thank him for all he does. His narcissistic self-praise is inadequate compensation for what he missed as a child. As president, Donald Trump makes the rest of us unsure about what he genuinely feels about America. He consistently makes Dreamers excessively anxious, perhaps getting them to feel the way he might have felt as a child, unsure whether his father would love him or send him packing. Trump now reverses his victim status by proposing the systematized destruction of countless families through mass deportation of darker-skinned Dreamers, decades after his father deported him—to NYMA.

While the media indulge in frequent speculation about whether Trump believes his lies, and even employ the term *lie* to describe his misstatements more frequently than any previous president in memory, rare indeed is the nonpartisan public figure who would identify Trump as a liar during the first months of his term. The collective silence of politicians—not just Republicans—has an enabling effect comparable to the role of the complicit parent of a deceptive child.

Psychoanalytic theory maintains that parents who allow their children's lies and self-deceptions to continue do so in order to avoid facing their own rapidly accumulating guilt that they didn't confront their children sooner. The longer they hold back, the harder it is to make the correction. The child observes this pattern and internalizes it, forgiving himself for lying and reinforcing his ability to deny his delinquency to himself. Trump's lies may be more widely discussed than those of any elected official in memory, but the tone in which they are often discussed contributes to the apparent ease with which he dismisses any such criticism and continues to speak his own unfounded version of the truth. Meanwhile, some of the most stable public figures are inhibited from calling Trump a liar because they are unconsciously doubling as parents trying to manage our infantile leader.

One speech pattern that has deservedly drawn attention to his conflicted relationship to the truth is his now-familiar tendency to attach the phrase "believe me" to his claims. Linguist Tyler Schnoebelen studied the 2016 campaign and reported that Trump uttered the phrase forty times during the presidential debates, often within statements that contained demonstrably inaccurate claims. When he was caught in a lie at the March 2016 AIPAC Policy Conference, eliciting laughter from the audience at his claim that he had studied the issue of the Middle East "in great detail, I would say actually greater by far than anyone else," he retorted, "Believe me. Oh, believe me," while the crowd was laughing at the audacity of his claim. Unconsciously, he fears ridicule and rejection because he knows he's making a false claim. Trump's trademark verbal tic serves as both a wish and a reassurance—revealing that he longs to believe what he says but cannot, even as he attempts to evade the addictive quality of his lying through the automatic repetition of the phrase with which he attempts to assert its truth. When he says "believe me," he's telling himself to believe himself—and unconsciously repeating what his parents must often have said to him when he was little.

Trump's lies inevitably have a corrosive effect on democracy and discourse. But lies aren't good for the liar either. Lying debilitates the ego and erodes one's capacity to reason. The pathological liar awards so much importance to the evasion of the truth that the process of maintaining the lie dominates other capacities to think. Fearing that he will be doubted, the liar thinks of various narratives that will materially support his lie, while internally he uses his lies to deny knowing the truth he is evading. So he cannot acknowledge a lie without undermining his inner need to avoid feeling responsible for his behavior. And ultimately the liar, who may at first seem smart and tricky, could in fact be starving his psyche, because pursuit of truth is as necessary to the mind as food is to the body, and without it the psyche starves.

One could certainly make the argument that the apparent

deterioration of Trump's verbal and mental capacities, which became such a popular topic of speculation late in 2017, is in fact the cumulative result of a lifetime of lying.

One characteristic of chronic liars is that they always embellish the truth, even when it's not necessary. Embellishment of the truth is compulsive and addictive. Chronic liars cannot *not* do it. Trump told Gwenda Blair he went to Fordham to be close to his parents, but his sister Maryanne had a different explanation—Fordham was where he got in. Trump rationalizes his lying when he thinks it's necessary, and shades or exaggerates even when it's not necessary. In this respect, lying has become second nature, a ubiquitous hallmark of his behavior. While the unconscious motivation is to manage anxiety and avoid feeling shame, in the long run lying has an opposite effect. Learning-disabled children, for example, learn early in childhood the effectiveness of exaggerating or inflating what they can do rather than getting dragged down by their challenges. But a lifelong pattern of such lies ultimately undermines any genuine feelings of confidence, because the individual knows that much of what he says about himself is at least partly fictitious. He can never feel genuine, belabored by the knowledge that his accomplishments are somehow superficial or are only about form and image. Without substance, we see why President Trump is so proud of his numerous executive orders and the things he thinks he's accomplished.

Because he cannot manage his anxiety without having to

lie on a daily basis, Trump has become a slave to his coping mechanism. Compulsive lying, however, prevents the individual from properly growing and maturing, which further limits his problem-solving capacities, making it harder to change. With his ability to think compromised by years of lying, he has little mental strength to draw upon to negotiate the bills involving the promises he made during the campaign, and limited understanding of such issues as health care and climate change, leaving him no option but to withdraw.

The longer he lies, the more difficult it is for Trump to see the world itself as real. In this respect, there is at least some relative truth in his catchall characterization of unwanted information as "fake news"—much of which simply doesn't comport with his fixed belief system, and thus on one level is experienced as "fake," or at least unreal. And "news" itself is threatening, because new knowledge poses a threat to his fixed ideas—making intelligence briefings, for example, not only hard to understand but also a danger to his psychic equilibrium. In that context, we can see how his reliance on omnipotent nostrums, especially his trademarked "Make America Great Again" mantra, offers strength through not only their exact content but also the security of predictability that comes through repetition.

What starts as an attempt to avoid anxiety by having to make an unwanted admission to himself eventually becomes more of an attack on self-knowledge. Over time he cannot tell truth from falsehood; rather than challenge his hyper-trophied sense of omniscience, he clings to whatever he says as true. The more he lies, the more he fears the truth, because admitting the truth could lead to psychic collapse.

As he lies to the world, he also lies to himself. On some level he knows this: the endless accusations of "fake news" are actually descriptions of the news he tells himself, not just us. He has so obfuscated his capacity to perceive reality—now internal reality—that he has no need to justify any of the lies he says. If he had that need, he would become anxious. Instead, he lies to himself to protect himself from anxiety—evading the pain, for example, that would have come from having to admit that the size of the crowd at his inauguration was less than half that of his African American predecessor, whose very citizenship Trump had questioned in a series of lies.

Trump's "fake news" accusations illustrate Trump's projecting onto others his own deceitful ways. But to fully appreciate the dynamics at play between lying and projection, we must return to one of Trump's most elaborate lies before entering political life—the ruse he perpetrated on the reporters he called in the 1980s claiming to be someone else. Multiple sources have confirmed that Trump repeatedly telephoned a series of reporters between 1980 and 1990 claiming to be a spokesman or colleague by the name of John Miller or John Barron, literally projecting himself into a false identity of his own creation. The subject of these conversations was invariably Donald Trump, whose praises "Miller" or "Barron" would sing. Usually the conversation was about Trump's success as a businessman or his desirability as a lover, and it was the exchanges that veered toward the latter that made the most distinct and lasting impressions. While some of the recipients of Trump's calls found the ruse "merely playful, if a bit weird," write Kranish and Fisher, other reporters "thought the calls were disturbing or even creepy, as [Trump] seemed to take pleasure in describing how prominent women were drawn to Trump sexually."

In the spring of 2018, however, the John Barron charade gained added resonance when a former *Forbes* reporter who helped assemble the Forbes 400 list of America's wealthiest revealed that Trump, as Barron, had lied his way onto that list. According to Jonathan Greenberg, writing in the *Washington Post* about his 1984 phone calls with John Barron, "Trump's fabrications provided the basis for a vastly inflated wealth assessment for the Forbes 400 that would give him cachet for decades as a triumphant businessman." Trump, as Barron, not only misrepresented the value of the Trump family's real estate holdings but also falsely asserted that by 1984 Fred Trump had already transferred the majority ownership of the family firm to Donald (who in fact had no equity in the firm until his father died in 1999). "The tactic landed him a place he hadn't earned on the Forbes list," concludes Greenberg, "and led to future accolades, press coverage and deals. It eventually paved a path toward the presidency."

The John Barron episode helped set into motion the

normalization that has developed around Trump's pathology. "Instead of believing that they were outright fabrications, my Forbes colleagues and I saw them simply as vain embellishments on the truth," Greenberg writes. "This was a model Trump would use for the rest of his career, telling a lie so cosmic that people believed that *some* kernel of it had to be real."

The normalization continues today. Psychologically healthy people do not assume false identities to spread lies about their deepest insecurities; instead, they assume that anyone who attempts such perfidy will be punished rather than rewarded. In a different set of circumstances, the reporting of Trump's every utterance would be legitimately qualified by a reminder of his history and propensity for such deceit; instead, the *Washington Post* measures his lies with the Pinocchio scale, trivializing their seriousness by measuring them with a children's cartoon image.

In John Barron's success at deceiving the news media, we see the seeds of both Trump's subsequent success at lying to the media in the decades that followed and his hostility toward the institution of an independent and fair free press. For all his attacks on the media, and his claims of being persecuted by the "fake news," he is aware that his John Barron ruse has never drawn the sustained public reprobation that it deserves, and his belief that he has gotten away with fooling journalists into believing he was someone else no doubt contributes to his contempt for the press. That contempt was already in full flower at the time of 1997's *The Art of the Comeback*. "People of the media are often recklessly devious and deceptive," he writes. "Recent polls have shown that the general public is wise to the act. Journalism—if you even want to call it that, these days—is widely considered one of the most untrustworthy professions in the United States." Trump knows he can't be trusted, and concludes that the media can't be trusted either; his attitude with the media is consistent with his projecting his untrustworthiness onto the media, and unconsciously using his untrustworthiness as a reason to discredit them.

The calls from John Barron or John Miller reportedly ended after he had to admit to the practice under oath in a 1990 lawsuit. But his perceived success at fooling people with a fake-identity ruse continued to resonate with him, as can be seen in his subsequent uses for the name Barron and its variations. Trump's "fascination with that name persisted for years," according to Kranish and Fisher, who note that when he was still married to Ivana he "sometimes used the code name 'the Baron' when he left messages for [then-mistress Marla Maples]." When Trump proposed a dramatic series based on his life and career to NBC in the wake of *The Apprentice*'s success, he wanted the character based on him to be named Baron. And of course, he and his third wife, Melania, named his third son Barron.

The use of the name for his fictitious self and for his son gains added resonance when considered in the context of where the name likely came from: Trump appears to have been introduced to the name Barron in his dealings with the Hilton heir he felt he bested in Atlantic City, and who he dismissed as a member of the "Lucky Sperm Club." Naming his son after a vanquished rival and his own alter ego reveals Trump's arrogant rejection of fact and his contempt for others, who he thinks never understood or appreciated who he really is. But it also underscores his need to believe that he can get away with the most essential lie he tells—that he is not who he is, not Donald Trump (but John Barron), and not a member of the "Lucky Sperm Club" (but a self-made billionaire). And by keeping alive the name at the center of the most elemental ruse he perpetrated on the media, he keeps alive his resentment toward not just the media but any institution that would deny him the opportunity to lie about his identity.

ELSEWHERE IN *The Art of the Comeback* Trump reveals how he projected his dishonesty not just onto the media but also in a business setting, writing that central to his ability to save himself from financial ruin was the message he "always sent out . . . : 'Don't lie to me. Don't cheat me. Because I'll find out and I'll find you and it won't be pretty.'" His hatred of being lied to is about as clear a projection as one could see. A cheater who knows in his heart that he's a cheat and can get away with it is going to unconsciously project his cheating and lying ways onto everyone he deals with. The projection protects him from having to admit to himself how much he lies—just as the harmless "truthful hyperbole" label reduces the impact of his dishonesty.

In what may be the ultimate expression of deception-related projection to come from Trump, he memorably responded to the publication of Wolff's *Fire and Fury* by reviving his calls to "toughen up libel laws" with the justification, "You can't say things that are false, knowingly false, and be able to smile as money pours into your bank account." Observers did not have to be well versed in the psychology of projection to appreciate that Trump was forbidding exactly what he has been doing for years—lying for profit.

The mention of other people's bank accounts highlights an important element of Trump's projection about lying. The association of finances and falsehoods isn't exactly new for him; after all, "truthful hyperbole" was initially justified as a "very effective form of promotion." When biographer Tim O'Brien reported that Trump wasn't worth as much as he claimed, Trump retaliated with a lawsuit seeking $5 billion in damages, but the suit ultimately backfired; under oath, Trump admitted in deposition that his claims about his wealth were based more on feelings than facts: "My net worth fluctuates, and it goes up and down with markets and attitudes and with feelings, even my own feelings." And Trump's insistence on keeping his tax returns private is widely believed to be an attempt to avoid revealing information that contradicts the public record about his personal finances.

Still, Trump's bringing up the bank account again in 2018 offered a remarkable glimpse into his likely unconscious thinking in response to a potentially existential threat to his presidency. Although Trump has been shown to have lied about a seemingly unlimited range of topics, he appears to have developed his capacity for untruthfulness initially and primarily in the business and financial world, where he was driven to outperform his father. On an unconscious level, the quest to surpass his father in business is in part an attempt to assert his independence from his mother, the original psychic wound that sets into motion the lifetime pattern of deception of the pathological liar.

To lie is to defy the law. Trump's habitual, pathological lying serves a number of unconscious functions: to express his deep-seated drive to defy the law; to assert his right to transcend the law; and to affirm his need to define himself outside the confines of the law. At a simple level, lying helps him get by in the world—and always has. The extent to which money has "poured into his bank account" over the years is, in his mind, a confirmation of his effectiveness and deservedness of successfully defining himself inside or outside of the law. Within weeks of winning the presidency, Trump was confronted with intelligence that suggested that past financial improprieties may have exposed him to Russian manipulation or even blackmail. If the allegations in the so-called Steele dossier are true, then his financial and legal survival will be determined by the success with which he continues to lie about where the money in his bank account came from. If Wolff's account of the Trump White House is true, then Trump's political survival will be determined by the success with which he continues to lie about the true motivation behind his presidential campaign. One thing is certain: where young Trump lied to assert himself, and businessman Trump lied to create himself, President Trump now lies to survive.

Chapter Six

THE PSYCHOLOGY OF NARCISSISM

There's no art to find the mind's
construction in the face.

— *William Shakespeare*

The only one that matters is me.
I'm the only one that matters.

— *President Donald J. Trump*

N arcissism, the most commonly used term to describe
Donald Trump's personality, can mean different things
to different people. Remarkably, virtually all definitions apply to
Donald Trump. To the general public, narcissism is a cluster of
behaviors that includes self-centered focus, lack of empathy, indifference to others, difficulty imagining the consequences of
one's actions, and shameless bragging. Narcissists manifest an
almost absolute degree of self-love, accompanied by an almost
total lack of self-awareness or awareness of their effect on

others. Narcissists show no interest in learning about themselves and think whatever they do is the best and most important thing anyone would ever want to do or accomplish.

Examples of Trump's narcissism are legion and instructive. A widely photographed instance occurred in February 2018, when Trump, boarding Air Force One on a rainy day, held a large umbrella to cover his head in the storm without inviting his wife or young son to join him. While depriving Melania and Barron of cover from the rain, Trump was exhibiting textbook signs of two kinds of narcissism: primary narcissism, associated with survival, which was the impulse behind his disregarding his family's comfort to ensure his own protection, and secondary narcissism, the impulse we connect to the familiar impulse to give oneself pleasure beyond mere survival—touching oneself, looking in the mirror—which drove his focus on keeping his hair in place in the storm.

A different storm brought out other sides to Trump's narcissism. Opening an August 2017 press conference in Corpus Christi during his trip to survey Hurricane Harvey's damage to Texas, Trump first had to comment on the size of the audience—"What a crowd! What a turnout!"—reminding observers that his self-centered impulse to see the world as a measure of his own reflection took priority over empathy and self-awareness. Days earlier, while the raging hurricane wrought havoc in Texas, Trump had announced his decision to pardon Joe Arpaio, the controversial and convicted racist sheriff from Arizona, which he acknowledged he had timed to coincide with "the middle of a hurricane, even though it was a Friday evening, [because] I assumed the ratings would be far higher than they were normally." By scheduling his announcement during a natural disaster, Trump demonstrated that his indifference to others' feelings was not subject to weather delays, a perverse twist on the credo of the postal service he oversees.

The many facets of Trump's narcissism have been widely chronicled, but less attention has been paid to its likely origins. Like so much of his pathology, Trump's narcissistic tendencies can be traced back to his earliest interactions in childhood. Narcissism stems from the baby's need for omnipotence, formed as a survival instinct in response to the absence of a fully nurturing and supportive connection to his mother. When feeling vulnerable or not cared for, young children retreat into a secret all-powerful world of grandiosity, where they feel protected from the inevitable hurts and disappointments of childhood. This can be a normal part of development, familiar to those of us who have children of our own. But some children deny even feeling hurt, having retreated already from an indifferent environment into their internally created world of safety. Other children feel enraged and betrayed whether or not the environment lets them down. But whatever the emotional response, narcissism is a defense created to maintain the grandiose self and remains the primary defense against any threats to the child's sense of omnipotence.

To that extent, narcissism is different from the Greek myth

from which it gets its name. In the myth, Narcissus was a handsome youth who fell in love with his refection while looking down in a lake; there's no mention of distant parents or other factors that would have made him vulnerable to having such a self-centered response to his reflection. Whatever the impetus, Narcissus was so enraptured by the beautiful face returning his gaze that he ceased to think of anything else, including eating. Eventually he weakened, fell into the lake, and drowned. The story is about obsessive self-love that ends in self-destruction, complete with an ironic and tragic ending that has transformed it into a cautionary tale that parents have long used to rein in their children.

There's a certain irony in the Narcissus myth's popularity among parents wanting to check their children's excessive self-regard, since narcissism can often be a reaction to a lack of early parental support, whether real or irrationally wished for. Trump's narcissism represents a compensatory response to deep injuries from his distant past; what reads as self-love is obscuring a profound need to be loved and admired by others, and a defense against any challenges to a grandiose sense of self that might make him feel vulnerable.

There are a variety of reasons why Trump would have retreated as a child to a state of omnipotent and destructive narcissism. Children naturally imitate their parents and eventually identify with them. At a deep level, young children think their parents are all-powerful and all-knowing. Trump certainly identified with both his father and mother, whose self-absorption is evident in family histories. The question is what happens when the child is disillusioned—or even worse, when parents disappoint or frighten their children. Donald Trump at some point learned that his mother was emotionally unavailable and that his father was absent and critical; combined with his own limited impulse control at school, which interfered with his traditional learning, these factors would contribute to a sense of despair over not getting enough warmth and meaningful nourishment from his earliest caretakers. This despair, in turn, would lead to narcissism, as a defense against shame and criticism, as well as against the need for any introspection that would cause him to face his selfish or hurtful behavior.

Narcissism begets a mind-set characterized by an aversion to depending on others that runs deep through many aspects of Trump's thinking. Adopting an attitude of indifference protects the narcissist from facing what psychoanalysts call "object hunger"—the human condition of needing other people—and obscures his facing the truth that even adults have dependency needs. Beneath the indifference and narcissism is a fear of dependency grounded in the notion that not being self-reliant is simply not acceptable to people as insecure as Donald Trump.

Not surprisingly, Trump's denial of his reliance on others flies in the face of his track record, which is filled with examples of his relying on others to get ahead. First his father's wealth got him started, of course, and kept him afloat when necessary. He was later bailed out of a potentially crippling lawsuit by Roy Cohn, who became the most influential adviser in Trump's life; gay and Jewish, Cohn also unconsciously served to embody Trump's ambivalence about having and needing a father figure, by personifying traits that Fred Sr. found unacceptable. Finally, television producer Mark Burnett lifted him from financial distress by making him a television star on *The Apprentice*. His bombastic self-made persona, meanwhile, gave no indication of any awareness that he had ever relied on anyone other than himself.

The illusion of independence fostered a sense of entitlement we see in his business life. Where his father built a fortune in part by maximizing his share of government assistance, Donald expertly manipulated zoning laws—another form of government assistance. Trump's mix of entitlement and grandiosity was so strong that he effectively denied his dependency on the vendors and contractors who worked on his buildings, famously paying a fraction of his contractual obligations—because paying in full would acknowledge that tradespeople could accomplish things that he needed and couldn't do himself. And the unfortunates to whom Trump owed money for services rendered made things worse for themselves just by demanding payment. Admitting that they needed him to pay his bills invited Trump's contempt; he recognized in them the unacceptability of his own dependence on others. Being able to project the fury he expresses at his own neediness onto others soothes and relieves him. Withholding money—Trump's favorite means of keeping score—makes him feel big and powerful in comparison, and expressing rage provides a physical release.

Trump no doubt benefited financially from not recognizing or honoring his debts—just as he benefited (if you can call it that) from evading so many unwanted truths or feelings. He essentially dehumanized himself. In his final years in business before entering politics, Trump externalized that dehumanization into his business sphere, transforming himself into a brand, his name disconnected from the work and risk that went into the construction projects bearing his imprimatur. In this latest business incarnation, Trump was able to avoid the responsibility for loss—receiving, and ultimately coming to expect, as great a reward for failure as for success.

Trump's resistance to paying bills and honoring contracts is symptomatic of another aspect of the narcissistic personality—a rejection of rules and regulations that apply to other people, and from which the narcissist asserts an immunity. A classic example of this can be found in his refusal to release his tax returns, asserting his exemption from the unofficial regulations by which his fellow candidates have historically abided. As Trump pointed out, he wasn't legally required by any rules to release his returns, despite years of accepted protocol that motivated other candidates to do so. By evoking the letter of the law to violate the spirit of its regulation, Trump was conveying his contempt for the construct of rules and regulations, and for the notion that he would be subject to their controls. From what little we know of what those tax returns are likely to reveal, they are themselves replete with contempt for regulation, likely expressed through finding loopholes in the tax system for his personal profit.

The narcissist's investment in his delusions of omnipotence is so pervasive and profound that he can psychologically ill afford to conceive of himself as governed by the rules and regulations that apply to lesser, less powerful people. Trump offered a glimpse of this mind-set when he claimed during a presidential debate that not paying taxes made him smart. The clear implication was that he was smarter than people who do pay taxes, superior to those who are burdened by any sense of responsibility for abiding by the rules and regulations that govern the less cunning. To a narcissist there is no concept of paying one's fair share to support government functions. The pitfalls of empowering an individual who thinks this way to run the government are self-evident.

We see a similar dynamic in Trump's success in turning bankruptcy laws into a way to manipulate the systems of legal and financial regulations for his personal profit. After his manic acquisition and spending spree in the late 1980s led to a series of bankruptcies in the 1990s, Trump famously maintained a lavish lifestyle while his creditors ended up paying the price, having to accept a fraction of their due on his debts. His debt was so vast and far-reaching that banks couldn't afford to hold him accountable; in a foreshadowing of the hold he would later claim on the Republican Party, Trump had made himself too big to fail. The question, now that Trump's tax reform dramatically increased America's national debt, is whether he has also made the United States itself too big to fail.

In his gaming of the bankruptcy system, Trump exhibited several previously discussed elements of his particular strain of narcissism. There's contempt for the notion that rules and regulations would apply to him. There's the assumption that he is entitled to more than his fair share when in fact he can't pay his debts. Spending his way into such a deep hole, he was likely in thrall to his delusions of omnipotence—which just as likely felt even less delusional when he emerged from the proceedings unscathed. The absence of any personal damage as a result of his corporate bankruptcies no doubt confirmed his narcissistic anti-dependency impulses as well.

Trump has been rebelling against rules and regulations since childhood, both in flagrant defiance of authority—the secret knife-buying trips to Manhattan that landed him in military school—and in subtler ways of maneuvering regulations to serve his agenda, such as when he "figured out all the angles" at summer camp. Unconsciously, sons experience having to follow rules as being castrated by the father: their fear of being castrated results from projecting onto their father their own wish to castrate him. Now, as president, he is arguably the world's most visible father figure, both responsible for and beholden to its most powerful rule-making and rule-enforcing apparatus. He is more pronouncedly in a position to castrate or be castrated—so far, only figuratively.

As his refusal to divest his business interests makes clear, Trump is still rebelling against rules and regulations, and using the system against itself—reminding observers that the absence of a provision against presidential conflicts of interest immunizes him by rendering such conflicts nonexistent by definition. Meanwhile, his law-and-order platform—enforced without mercy on immigrant families, for example—demonstrates his willingness to deploy the system against others. Of course, the laws of the United States—specifically, its election laws and Electoral College—are the source of his power today, even if he may have illegally influenced them. The narcissistic impulse to identify as self-created—to deny any other influence or input in the narcissist's progression toward omnipotence—adds another unconscious impetus to Trump's need to justify his disregard for the law, or at least its application to him. Not only are his delusions of omnipotence unlikely to be abandoned, but he is now frighteningly well positioned and psychically motivated to defend and even realize them.

When contemplating the potentially devastating costs of unchecked narcissism, particularly in an individual with as much access to damage-wielding power as Donald Trump, it can be tempting to forget that the narcissistic impulse has its origins in a defensive, compensatory response. Infant observation researchers have traced the formation of the omnipotent conception of the self to the young baby's struggle to survive when not in his mother's care. The infant experiences the unintegrated parts of his personality as lacking a "binding force between themselves," writes psychoanalytic theorist Joan Symington; these disparate personality aspects, she continues, are experienced as being "held together passively in a very precarious way by a psychic skin, equated with the physical skin." In the baby's primitive understanding, this imagined skin becomes the only protection from a "constant danger of suddenly spilling out in a state of unintegration, should this fragile psychic skin be breached or lost." This "desperate survival measure," which is echoed in adulthood by the "same sorts of survival mechanisms, over and over again at times of crisis," can set the individual on a psychic course that leads from infantile fears of chaos through primitive and defensive delusions of omnipotence to full-blown narcissism.

The notion of the psychic skin provides a helpful construct for organizing and understanding a variety of the now-familiar defenses in Trump's pathology. While common to all of us, moments of early childhood desperation are more of a factor when the mother is absent or disengaged, so young Donald likely had ample need and opportunity to develop the defenses that Symington describes. The child in a family where parental holding and understanding are in short supply will discover new mechanisms for holding himself together. Often, the infant searching for a protective, containing source of comfort "may engage in constant bodily movement which then feels like a continuous holding skin," Symington writes. Young Donny's incessant muscular activity—which came to include neighborhood behavior that today reads as childhood aggression—accrues something approaching poignancy when viewed as a desperate attempt to soothe himself.

In adulthood, Trump has developed a variety of less poignant pursuits that have served the function of containing and comforting psychic skin. Power, money, sexual conquests, publicity, and the proliferation of self-named towers and products around the world have all at various times helped him organize his inner space to defend against chaos. Perhaps none of these was as effective as starring as a reality television version of himself in *The Apprentice*. Watching the Donald Trump of *The Apprentice* gave Trump the chance to see himself on the screen as a fully integrated, authoritative, effective individual—who, in this version, wasn't struggling to recover from a series of near-disaster corporate bankruptcies. The show's ratings success was a bonus, as was the unique opportunity to behold his psychic skin made visible for the world to see. But as with so many matters involving Trump, the most important viewer metric was an audience of one, Trump himself. Seeing a Donald Trump who could disregard his financial troubles, operate in a fake and idealized version of his world, and earn deference and adoration by exhibiting unchallenged agency and the ability to fire people at will worked as a restorative and empowering therapy unmatched by all of Trump's previous attempts to integrate and contain himself. One wonders if Trump would have had the mental strength to imagine himself as President Trump if he hadn't first been *Apprentice* star Trump. It would have been just what the doctor ordered—had there been a doctor, and if a doctor could have imagined such a thing.

Unfortunately, like so many narcissism-based defenses, the relief offered by the digital psychic skin of *The Apprentice* was only temporary. Recalling Jacques Lacan's theories of the mirror stage, we're reminded that the infant who gazes upon the reflection of his fully integrated self is presented with both a vision of the level of integration to which he aspires and a reminder that internally he feels that he perpetually falls short of the integration he sees in the mirror. Donald Trump knows he is no "Donald Trump," and that the TV version of himself—who turned "You're fired!" into a catchphrase for viewers who fantasized about having so much agency in their own lives—would never be so cowardly as to resort to firing his cabinet secretaries by tweet. That's why I was scarcely surprised when an acquaintance shared with me the previously unreported discovery she made while on a private White House tour that Barron Trump offered a classmate and her family. In a room off the Oval Office, which had been outfitted with several large-screen TVs, the group discovered none other than the president, watching reruns of himself on *The Apprentice*. Trump still needs the comfort of seeing himself made whole by a televised second skin, even if it reminds him that he still doesn't feel that wholeness inside.

Now he derives the comfort of a psychic skin from his rallies, where the adoration of the crowd chanting his name confirms the better image of himself that he doesn't in fact feel, and the public cabinet meetings and signing ceremonies, where again he is buoyed by affirming adoration, if on a smaller scale. Although, like so many idiosyncrasies of the Trump presidency, they have been normalized by observers, neither first-year campaign rallies nor fawning cabinet meetings staged as performance art have precedent in previous administrations; observers perhaps understand they are performing some necessary function for the president, without knowing precisely what that is. His "executive time"—reportedly spent tweeting while binge-watching Fox News and eating fast food—and his endless rounds of golf also offer adult iterations of the repetitive continuous movements that are observed in infants seeking the containing function.

His narcissistic needs require so much continuous support that he also seeks it in private, out of the public eye. He is on the phone every evening talking with numerous business associates and acquaintances. He holds small private dinners at the White House, attended by a variety of loyalists ranging from Oracle exec Safra Catz and venture capitalist Peter Thiel to staffers Corey Lewandowski and Kellyanne Conway. He hosts Sarah Palin, Kid Rock, and Sean Hannity. They praise him, listen to him, and agree about his greatness, providing external reinforcement to the ever-endangered integrity of that psychic skin.

There are limits to how effective the psychic skin approach to self-treatment can be. Former economic adviser Gary Cohn, in an email quoted in *Fire and Fury,* offered an assessment of President Trump that evokes Symington's description of the unstructured, uncontained infant: "Trump is less a person than a collection of terrible traits." That collection of impulses and resentments requires an impenetrably thick skin to contain it. It's no coincidence that Trump wants to build a wall—he has created an internal psychological wall that will repel and protect him from emotional connection with the outside world. When he promises to "drain the swamp," he is revealing an unconscious fantasy of his mental insides, and the emotional glue that holds him together.

Beyond the limitations of its efficacy, the psychic-skin defense places constraints on the individual's internal mental space in which to think. As that space becomes organized into good and bad experiences, it remains two-dimensional; the thought process doesn't evolve to three-dimensional levels of complexity, and the fear of opening an insides-draining gap prevents new ideas from finding an entry point. We see how difficult it is for Trump to listen—even when *I hear you* is written on his instruction card—and he either blocks out or mimics what others say (or what is written on his card to reiterate). When he speaks he repeats himself, latching on to set phrases like "no collusion," "fake news," and "believe me." His speech betrays evidence of limited capacity, including perseveration, such as when he repeats favored topics, like rigged elections or the death of DACA, and echolalia, as when he repeats phrases he hears on Fox News, a two-dimensional medium with which he has a powerful but primitive relationship, without any apparent knowledge of what these phrases mean.

Understandably, these limitations help explain why the psychic-skin defense and "other omnipotent defense mechanisms," as Symington notes, will "further block emotional development." As a result, Trump is maintaining an omnipotent position that may keep "echoes of the very early unheld precariousness" at bay, which "in turn motivates the patient to hold himself together." But he never grows or transforms into something new, creative, or different. His refusal to face reality's limitations contributes to his static personality, which he admits is virtually unchanged since childhood. Trump is all about holding, like having a plaster cast that holds parts of his mind together—or at least keeps them ready for tweeting, golf, television, or signing executive orders.

This kind of arrested development brings us back to the myth from which Trump's narcissism got its name: the myth of Narcissus ends with his death, because he was focused so exclusively on his reflection that he forgot to eat. The message was clear: unchecked self-love becomes self-destruction, regardless of whether it is intentional. Trump's psychic starvation parallels Narcissus's physical starvation; so in love was he that seeing his name on tall buildings replaced curiosity about his inner world. He has lost an ability to think, to listen, or to make sense of his environment in terms that are anything other than fundamentally narcissistic—that is, what can the environment do for him?

That focus is also closely aligned with greed, narcissism's handmaiden. Greed is stimulated by excessive envy, driven by a desire to have and consume everything, especially things that might arouse spiteful envy in others. Trump famously claimed in *The Art of the Deal* that his deal-making drive was not motivated by greed, but events have clearly proven otherwise. Although he would no doubt deny it, Trump's powerful greed also extends beyond material possessions to qualities he envies in others. Unconsciously, greed can be traced back to the infant's ambivalence toward the bountiful breast—simultaneously relying on its providing nurture and sustenance while resenting its seemingly inexhaustible goodness. Now in his capacity as the head of government (functionally, the keeper of the national breast), Trump wants unconsciously to deplete its resources, suck it dry and keep the goodness for himself and his cronies. In this respect—depleting and destroying the government that empowers him—greed can serve as an unintentional weapon for Trump's narcissistic self-destruction. But the rest of us become collateral damage.

Another path to self-destruction awaits the narcissist who falls under delusions of grandiosity. Long before he floated the ideas of military parades or a presidency for life, Trump behaved as president less like a servant of the state than like the *embodiment* of the state. Apparently surprised that he can't execute his office with the absolute authority of a Mafia boss, Trump seems dissatisfied with being the most powerful man on earth. Aspiring to a greater power, he brings to mind the unconscious grandiosity reminiscent of what psychoanalyst Ernest Jones described over a century ago in "The God Complex."

To read Jones today is to confront the question of how he could have envisioned Trump's Twitter feed in 1913. To the individual who has been afflicted with the God complex, Jones writes, "even the most trivial pieces of information about himself, those which an ordinary man sees no object in keeping to himself, are invested with a sense of high importance, and are parted with only under some pressure." Also applicable to Trump, he writes that communication "is often not written at all, but instead is constantly hinted at with repeated promises that it will be disclosed on a further occasion." Trump has become known for his grandiose promises, as well as for his vague "we'll see" comments when he can't answer a question.

But the opposite of "we'll see" is when Trump jumps to conclusions from a shred of information, such as when he treated as absolute fact one Fox News statement that Obama tapped telephones at Trump Tower. Trump's unconscious fantasy of omniscience feeds his resistance to accepting new knowledge unless it fits his presuppositions. Grandiose people never apologize or express remorse for something they did. Nor do they admit fallibility in their words or memory;

Trump—of the "very good brain" and "one of the great memories of all time"—will defend his memory as perfect even in light of contradictory statements a day prior or hence. To Trump, anything is true the moment he says it, simply because he says it.

Trump's infallibility applies to the future as well; predictions are important to individuals with the God complex. They will keep predicting something positive, like Trump's saying that he will "make America great again." This reveals a psychotic fantasy of having an unconscious sense of power over future time. They promise something great, but they also predict something disastrous if they are not listened to or if their ideas are not followed.

Trump famously appropriated Reagan's campaign slogan—"Let's make America great again"—when it was time to come up with his own. The one-word difference between the two slogans is telling. Eliminating the word *let's*, while coupling it with the sentiment behind his infamous declaration "I alone can fix it," makes it clear who is doing the making when it comes to greatness. This is especially evident when the slogan is paired with his name, as in so many campaign materials that effectively read "Trump Make America Great Again." Trump appears to be making a conscious effort to position himself as a savior; on some level, of course, he knows that saviors' stories rarely end well, and unconsciously the role he is creating for himself is that of martyr—which is exactly the role he would have assumed had he lost the election as reportedly intended.

Having won the election, however, any intimated aspirations to the role of the martyred savior inevitably will lead him—and us—on a path toward a more profound and damaging self-destruction.

To avoid the self-destruction that is the endpoint of narcissism, President Trump needs to externalize what would otherwise be an internally vital threat to his survival—the investigation into his campaign's possible collusion with Russian interference into the election. What began as a probe into the possibility that Trump had committed his arguably biggest act of narcissistic omnipotence yet—assuming he could get away with treason—has expanded into a broader investigation of seemingly unrelated legal and financial issues that would have compromised him and his family with the Russians. As his second year in office found him squarely in the target and narrowing focus of the Mueller investigative team, Trump's survival increasingly hinged on keeping his latest threatening father figure at bay, hiding his delinquent financial dealings, and protecting his fragile self. One way for him to externalize self-destruction is to encourage outside groups to attack each other—or at least to stay out of the way when attacks flare up between Democrats and Republicans, immigrants and nativists, whites and blacks. Considered from this angle, the divisiveness Trump has fomented in our culture can be seen as his defense against the narcissist's fate. A similar dynamic plays out as Trump pushes his self-destructive impulses into government itself, getting the judiciary to destroy government institutions and cabinet members to destroy the very agencies they are supposed to direct.

We see just how dangerous President Trump is when he projects his self-destructive impulses into the government, because on a profound psychic level, he believes he is the government. Destroying the government and the nation thus becomes both the defense and the thing defended against—both protection and destruction. Students of history may see echoes of the Vietnam-era policy of destroying the village to save the village, a reminder of the enormous damage that can be inflicted by misguided leadership. It's tempting to comfort oneself with the notion that checks and balances will prevent Donald Trump from inflicting too much damage to the nation in his perhaps inevitable narcissistic reckoning. No such comfort can be taken without first giving serious consideration to this simple question: Which prospect is likely more frightening to Donald Trump, revealing his tax returns or starting a nuclear war?

Chapter Seven

THE PSYCHOLOGY OF DESTRUCTIVENESS

I can go back into my office and pick up the
telephone and in 25 minutes 70 million people
will be dead.

—President Richard M. Nixon

The habituating narcotic of hate destroys all the
good things that, together, we stand for.

—former Speaker of the House Jim Wright
(D-TX)

Donald Trump came to the presidency as a builder, a
real estate mogul who constructed and put his name
on hotels, casinos, luxury high-rise residential towers, and re-
sorts around the world. He built an empire surpassing his father's; instead of putting the family name on a middle-class
village in Brooklyn, he attached it to a high-end tower in Manhattan. Trump later expanded his success as a builder into a
multipurpose brand, plastering his name on a wide variety of

commercial products and enterprises, and transforming his persona into a character presented as "Billionaire Donald Trump" on the hit television series *The Apprentice*. Later, as his 2016 campaign-season victories mounted and his unlikely political successes grew steadily in number, he positioned himself as the builder of a movement, who claimed he could do with human resources what he had prided himself on achieving with construction materials.

Trump came to the presidency as a destroyer as well. He vanquished his GOP rivals for the nomination with startling efficiency. He exploded protocol, defied norms, disregarded convention, broke rules and perhaps laws, and encouraged similar behavior among the men and women who made up the movement he built. He also left a trail of destruction along the path that led him to politics—bankruptcies, divorces, broken deals, abandoned and empty buildings, and personal fortunes lost by individuals who put their trust and faith in his word, his brand, and the fantasies he sold to the gamblers whose losses funded his casinos. As president, he has dismantled federal agencies and rolled back consumer protections. He has hacked away at the Environmental Protection Agency, taken back public lands to facilitate commercial development, and abolished net neutrality.

All of us are driven by conflicting urges to build and to destroy. Both are powerful inborn drives, competing for dominance in the personality for the entirety of our lives. Freud observed both of them as operative in the determinative drives that he labeled the life instinct and the death instinct. As noted earlier, Melanie Klein saw both drives as present and influential beginning in the earliest stages of infancy. The infant's earliest attempts to manage his destructive drives are central to Klein's concept of the formation of the personality, which she traces back to the baby's limited initial experience and understanding of the world in general and his mother or other essential caregiver in particular. The baby's unconscious management of his destructive impulses, in Klein's formulation, can shape his personality for life, and is sensitive to his particular dynamics with his mother. Trump's enormous capacity for destruction, at times more prevalent than his more traditionally celebrated ability to build and construct, is seen in sharper relief when viewed as the adult expression of the lifelong failure to manage his unconscious destructive impulse to destroy.

In Klein's model, the reader will recall, the destructive drive is the central and most powerful impulse that the infant must contend with in his earliest interactions with the world. The baby develops the primitive mechanisms of splitting and projection in order to feel like he has gotten rid of the most destructive aspects of his personality. Nevertheless, the process of splitting and projection is imperfect, and the baby is left with ongoing psychic anxiety that the bad parts of the self will destroy the good parts—anxiety that requires management early on by the infant as well as by his family. The mother plays the central role in that management. If the mother is present and affectionate, then the baby learns how to take the unconscious mental steps that will allow him to change his anxiety into something he can tolerate. But if the dynamic between mother and infant is challenged—by the mother's absence, for example, or the infant's hyperactivity—then the baby remains influenced by fear and by an impulse to oversimplify his world.

What little we know about Mary Trump's life at the time of Donald's infancy and early childhood points to the strong possibility that she was not able to provide needed assistance in managing his infantile psychic anxiety about his inner destructiveness. If Mrs. Trump, the former domestic and nanny who married into a household that allowed her to employ her own servants, exhibited an especially warm or maternal character in the raising of her children, it has not been reported. The few details that we do know about her life during her child-raising years point to a mother who was distant, if not absent, limited by her health, and likely ill-equipped to deal with a fussy, fidgety baby who would grow into an aggressive, hyperactive child.

Donald Trump, meanwhile, displays multiple hallmarks in adulthood of an unintegrated destructive impulse that was not managed in infancy or childhood. He seems unable to appreciate the complexity of either the external world or his internal life; unwilling or incapable of even considering that his behavior might originate from his own destructive impulses, he instead projects those impulses onto his persecutors, who in his perspective are legion. His own fallibility, liability, and accountability are too dangerous for him to consider and must be denied to maintain his chances of survival.

Sometimes Trump seems almost to get stuck in attack mode, or to go on the attack in circumstances when a less aggressive approach might be expected to serve him better; his attacks on Gold Star families, for example, have defied all expectations, first when he starts the fights with survivors of military men killed in action, then when he doubles down and elevates hostilities rather than retreats. His first public fight with a Gold Star family—the parents of fallen Army Captain Humayun Khan—erupted into an unlikely Twitter war following Khizr and Ghazala Khan's July 2016 appearance at the Democratic National Convention. At the time, the alarming degree of hostility that Trump leveled at the Khans was ascribed to the high tensions characterizing the final months of a hard-fought campaign. The following October, however, Trump got into another fracas, this time with the pregnant widow of a soldier killed on his watch—Army Sergeant La David Johnson, one of four Green Berets slain in Niger, a country most Americans didn't realize had a US military presence until news of the ambush surfaced. Details of the raid—including the two-day lapse between the attack and the discovery of Johnson's remains—were still emerging when Trump placed a condolence call to Johnson's widow, but the call didn't go well; Myesha Johnson reported that Trump seemed to forget her husband's name and that he suggested Johnson "knew what he signed up for," a remark that was at best tone-deaf given the circumstances. When Johnson went public with her anger over the call, Trump got more defensive, and accused Johnson of misrepresenting their discussion. The spectacle of Trump fighting publicly with the pregnant widow of a soldier killed in action on his watch invited speculation that Trump didn't back down simply because he couldn't. One of the soldiers was Muslim and the other was African American.

At a White House ceremony later that same week, he interrupted prepared remarks to attack Senator Elizabeth Warren (calling her "Pocahontas" during a tribute to Navajo Code Talkers) and then taunted Kim Jong Un, calling him "Little Rocket Man" while selling his tax break as "rocket fuel" for the economy. Rarely has Trump seemed less capable of curbing his impulses both to destroy his targets and risk collateral damage as he thoroughly undermined his efforts to celebrate Native Americans and to cultivate security in the economy, respectively. Projection continues to play a role in Trump's attacks, as he could be called "Big Rocket Man"; on a still deeper level, he is likely projecting his own fears of being "little Donny" onto Kim Jong Un.

Trump's frequent, sometimes mystifying attacks, assaults, and abuses can begin to make more sense when viewed through the lens of the unmodulated destructive impulse. Of the wide variety of forms that the innate destructive drive can take, some are obvious expressions of a drive to destroy, such as Twitter assaults, like "Lightweight Senator Kirsten

Gillibrand . . . who would come to my office begging for campaign contributions not so long ago (and would do anything for them)" and "It's a shame what's happened with the FBI," which he earlier tweeted was "in tatters." When an attack is an expression of innate destructiveness, the object of the attack can be virtually immaterial; rather, the simple act of attacking reflexively fulfills a deep-seated need that can preclude conscious thought. As in infancy, the adult whose destructive impulse has never been brought under control can unconsciously call upon the destructive drive in response to a wide variety of stimuli, from feelings of helplessness and inner chaos to threats of abandonment or neglect. The identity of the person or institution on the receiving end of the destructive impulse may reveal less about what is going on in the individual's unconscious than the circumstances to which the destructive outburst can be seen as a response. As we'll see, an examination of what precipitates Trump's destructive outbursts can reveal patterns of predictability.

It's worth considering again how the destructive impulse is first experienced—in the chaotic jumble of early infancy. Driven by primitive conflicting impulses toward his mother—alternately to punish her for causing discomfort and to preserve her as a source of nourishment—the baby experiences anxiety about his capacity to destroy the thing he loves and relies on most. From this conflict develops a faint recognition of the need to manage his aggressive and destructive impulses. The discomfort of confronting his own limitations often inspires aggressive fantasies of attacking the caregivers on whom he depends. These destructive fantasies usually begin to disappear by the end of childhood, as the infant's delusions of omnipotence are modified by the limitations of reality—a process central to intellectual growth and development. But for some individuals who fail to outgrow the infant's defenses of splitting and projection, and thus never develop the capacity to feel concern about hurting a loved one, this primitive, pre-moral destructiveness can persist well into adulthood, accompanied by an unconscious process that helps them cope by never having to recognize any feelings of actually being destructive.

Projection is common, natural, and in and of itself neutral, but it is a primitive mechanism with only limited efficacy. Seeing oneself as either good or bad—and projecting the latter capacity outside the self to preserve the illusion of the former—can only work for so long. Being able to see oneself as good *and* bad—constructive and destructive—is a necessary next step toward developing a healthy and integrated person. The goal is to acknowledge, live with, and learn from anxiety rather than just try to deny it by evacuating or outsourcing it. The dynamic between infant and mother plays a central and influential role in that development, and deficiencies in that dynamic can result in the child growing up too reliant upon the projection defense, unprepared to acknowledge and accept his capacity for destruction and unable to modify the anxiety that inevitably accompanies it.

Donald Trump is a clear illustration of what projection looks like in an adult who has never learned to temper it as a primitive tool he acquired in infancy. The most obvious and familiar examples are the nicknames he gives opponents—"Crooked Hillary," "Lyin' Ted," and "Pocahontas" Elizabeth Warren, all flagrant attempts to associate others with his own denied tendencies to indulge in unethical practices, engage in serial prevarication, and misrepresent his origins, respectively. (The wealthy German American heir's attempts to represent himself as a self-made Swedish American is of course every bit as deserving of critical examination as Warren's claims to be part Native American.) Trump's nicknaming of his opponents are textbook projections, clear instances of an individual accusing another of having the same destructive tendencies and character defects that he wants to deny in himself.

Trump's birther campaign against Barack Obama—his first foray into a serious run at the US presidency—was also constructed around a series of projections. The doubt that Trump sought to cast upon Obama's origins can be seen as an expression of his anxiety about the gap between his self-made image and his privileged upbringing. The charge that his classmates don't remember Obama in the grade school he attended echoed a revelation that David Cay Johnston reports in *The Making of Donald Trump*: "Others have said they don't recall seeing Trump a lot around campus," Johnston writes of Trump's college years, "an interesting observation in view of Trump's claims years later that 'nobody remembers seeing' future President Barack Obama in elementary school in Hawaii or anywhere else." And of course the sinister meaning he assigned to Obama's keeping his birth certificate private presages his subsequent fears of revealing his own government documentation, the tax returns he refuses to make public. He insisted Obama show his "long form" birth certificate and not simply a "short form"—terms generally reserved for tax returns.

As president, Trump's reliance on the projection defense remains pronounced, as when he proclaimed, for example, that "we have a lot of sickness in some of our institutions" as he traveled to the Florida Panhandle to campaign for accused pedophile and Alabama senator candidate Roy Moore. He can often be witnessed committing the same slights of which he accuses the Democrats, such as when he complains that they shun his overtures but then fails to invite Jewish Democrats to the White House Hanukkah party, or when he blamed Democrats for backing away from DACA when he was the one who ended the program. During the Obama administration, Trump repeatedly criticized the president for spending so much time playing golf; in his first year in office, Trump spent more time on the course than any POTUS in history. And the accusations of "fake news" that he hurls so belligerently at stories that displease him can be seen as vivid examples of the drive to project one's destructive impulses outside the self.

Trump was attempting to manage his destructive impulses through projection long before he entered politics, however. A remarkable illustration emerges in a discussion of his acquisition of Mar-a-Lago from the Marjorie Merriweather Post Foundation in *The Art of the Comeback*:

> *On the Post Foundation sat various members of Marjorie Merriweather Post's family, among them Dina Merrill, Mrs. Post's arrogant and aloof daughter, who was born with her mother's beauty but not her brains. During my fight to save Mar-a-Lago, Merrill would constantly criticize me and say things behind my back, all of which would get back to me. She should have been the one to save Mar-a-Lago, Mommy had given her the money, and it would have been an easy and popular thing to have done. Instead she lives in a terribly furnished Palm Beach condominium, thinking about her failed acting career and how she can make me look as "nouveau" as possible.*

Trump clearly goes out of his way here to convey his contempt for Dina Merrill—enough to suggest that he was perhaps plagued by guilt over some aspect of the transaction, which won him the West Palm Beach estate for a fraction of its value. He characterizes his predatory efforts to acquire the National Historic Landmark as a noble attempt to "save" Mar-a-Lago. Perhaps he experienced guilt because the terms of the deal were so unfavorable to the foundation—a nonprofit philanthropic organization, which had previously attempted to donate the property to the government to serve as a winter White House.

Perhaps he envied that the fortune Dina Merrill's "mommy" left behind was substantially greater than that which his "daddy" had left him; note that he references Mrs. Post's legacy as merely "brains and beauty." Perhaps he dismissed Dina Merrill's elegant, antique-filled home as "terribly furnished" because his preferences in decor and furnishings were mercilessly ridiculed by tastemakers of the day. Trump's own paranoid anxiety, potentially laced with elements of self-awareness, comes through in his fear that she would successfully devalue him with the "nouveau riche" label.

A studied consideration of the passage leads to the interpretation that Trump attacks Merrill with such contempt because he has projected the disavowed part of himself onto her—and almost says as much at the end of the paragraph. The contempt is consistent with a fear that Merrill would see who Trump "really" was, and tell the world that no amount of spending would allow the tough-talking Queens native with the heavy outer-borough accent to achieve the elegant veneer he desired to present to the world. That fear has been a primary motivator his entire life.

Envy is a fundamental source of the destructive impulse. While projection is the psychic-defense mechanism that plays the most central role in the individual's effort to manage anxiety about his destructive impulses, it is inextricably linked in infancy with envy—in ways that, we'll see with Trump, continue well into adulthood. Envy originates at the breast, as the baby derives love, nourishment, comfort, security, warmth from the breast—or from the mother's intimate use of the bottle accompanied by physical closeness and maternal warmth. But there is no way the mother can always gratify the baby, and if these disappointments and absences are long, the baby feels the breast is depriving him and keeping all the good milk inside. The baby is angry, feels destructive, and may even refuse the next feed for a while because of paranoid fear that the breast will attack it (deriving from the baby's defensively projecting his bad feelings and rage onto the breast).

When in these circumstances the baby comes to understand the breast as being mean and withholding, then destructive fantasies and impulses ensue, such as biting the breast, or turning away in an attempt to hurt the mother and spoil her loving efforts to repair any harm she might have done to her baby by being away or otherwise occupied. Envy evolves over time into a malicious attitude toward another person's good fortune. It leads to fantasies of destroying the good (whether wealth, reputation, looks, or relationships), as a result of hating the pain caused by the "feeling that someone else enjoys something desirable," as Melanie Klein put it in *Envy and Gratitude*. What is envied are literal and figurative possessions (money, power) and qualities (decency, thoughtfulness, fulfillment, character strength), and the pain of not having those leads to impulses to either take them away or destroy them.

In fantasy, envy is experienced as a feeling of "sour grapes," but in action it can be seen in Trump's commitment to taking away access to affordable health insurance roles and even poisoning America's love for Obama's generosity of spirit and his palpable accomplishments. Trump wants to destroy these remnants of Obama's legacy, unconsciously aware that he lacks—or at least that he is seen to lack—Obama's strength of character, compounded by his awareness that a majority of American citizens regard Trump as a delinquent liar.

Trump's unchecked envy of Obama has already been massively destructive—he has rolled back major regulations installed by Obama to protect everything from our environment to schools to the judiciary. Trump is attempting to fill US district courts with unqualified young lawyers who will remain on the bench for decades to come. Envy often goes with greed, as Trump greedily claims any success Obama had, for example with unemployment, as his own. Finally, envy sufficiently diminishes the image of the envied person so he never again could contain anything enviable.

Envious people hate needing others, which implies dependency, and acknowledges that others may have possessions or attributes that the envious individual lacks. The story of young Donald gluing together and thus appropriating younger brother Robert's building blocks suggests that Trump may have been operating from a position of envy his entire life. By keeping Robert's blocks, Donald was expressing his envy of Robert for replacing Donald as the baby. Such envy would prevent Donald from appreciating Robert's goodness—the generosity that led him to let Donald use his blocks in the first place—and set

Donald on a path of attacking and spoiling the good in others. Robert may have been simply overwhelmed, helpless in the face of his big brother. But even then Donald thought that what someone else had was rightfully his.

Trump's destructiveness also fuels his deep drive to exact revenge on people he feels hurt him. Revenge is a defense against many forms of weakness—shame, loss, guilt, powerlessness, and mourning. The drive to exact revenge is fueled by a sense that the individual is entitled to pursue retribution for perceived harms inflicted by the other. Any guilt the revenge seeker might feel is overridden by a sense of getting back what's due, and by narcissistic rage attempting to restore feeling grandiose.

Trump describes his taste for vengeance in unapologetic, biblical terms in *The Art of the Comeback.* "I believe in an eye for an eye—like the Old Testament says," he writes. "Some of the people who forgot to lift a finger when I needed them, when I was down, they need my help now, and I am screwing them against the wall. I'm doing a number . . . and I'm having so much fun. People say that's not nice, but I really believe in getting even."

Trump gives the title "Revenge" to a chapter in his self-help tome *Think Big*; when he opens the chapter with the bold statement "I always get even," what's remarkable is the simple clarity of his claim—no sign of worry or guilt. Revenge allows him easily to justify to himself his willful destructiveness; by defining himself as a counterpuncher, he can claim his aggression is always reactive. He justifies the reactive stance in part by projecting his own destructiveness onto others. When he was on the lecture circuit, "earning $100,000 per appearance at motivational seminars hosted by Tony Robbins," according to Kranish and Fisher, he told a St. Louis audience that "paranoia was crucial to success. 'Now that sounds terrible,' Trump said. 'But you have to realize that people—sadly, sadly—are very vicious. You think we're so different from the lions in the jungle?'" Johnston quotes another of Trump's speeches from his days as a motivational speaker in which he revealed the pleasure he takes in matching the aggression he sees in the world with his own hostility: "If somebody screws you, you screw 'em back ten times over. At least you can feel good about it. Boy, do I feel good. . . . I love getting even when I get screwed by someone—yes, it is true. . . . Always get even. When you are in business you need to get even with people who screw you. You need to screw them back fifteen times harder . . . go for the jugular, attack them in spades!"

What Trump is describing here is revenge that stems from narcissistic injury. Central to that rage are the ideas of righting a wrong and undoing a hurt—the latter of which is inevitably a grandiose fantasy, because hurt cannot ever be undone. Somewhat more realistically, Trump pursues revenge in order to put his hurt in perspective and move on; he appears to be incapable of putting slights and injuries behind him until he has extracted his pound of flesh. He seeks to accomplish this by reversing his humiliation—humiliating the humiliator—avoiding anything that evokes memories of being mocked or duped as a child, which can come along when he has to face facts or look in the mirror.

One of Trump's more high-profile retaliations was against Malcolm Forbes, after *Forbes* magazine called his wealth into question by lowering his rank on their listing of the world's wealthiest men. Trump responded by exacting personal revenge in *Surviving at the Top*. "It always amazed me that people pay so much attention to *Forbes* magazine," he writes. "Often, how well you fared on that list depended greatly on the state of your personal relationship with the editor, the late Malcolm Forbes," with whom Trump acknowledges he "did not have a good relationship":

> *At one time Malcolm and I had gotten along just fine; we chatted amiably at parties and occasionally talked on the phone. But I gradually came to see him as a hypocrite who favored those who advertised in his magazine and tried, with surprising viciousness, to punish those who didn't. I also saw a double standard in the way he lived openly as a homosexual—which he had every right to do—but expected the media and his famous friends to cover for him. Malcolm and the Forbes family no doubt sensed my coolness toward them, and for that reason, and also because I never advertised much in Forbes magazine, they were not great admirers of Donald Trump. In retrospect, I can see it was*

only a matter of time before the family started using its
magazine against me.

Trump is engaging in some obvious projection here—the "surprising viciousness" he ascribes to Forbes is clearly his own, as is the impulse to use one's publication against a perceived enemy. Also worth noting is the structure of his initial critique of the publication, framed as his being "amazed . . . that people pay attention to" *Forbes* and its wealth ranking— an attempt to mask his envy as contempt, when in fact it is a direct expression of contempt disavowed. Perhaps most remarkable is his switching mid-sentence from first person to third—likely an unconscious attempt to protect himself from facing the probability that the Forbes family didn't like him personally, not just for not advertising in the magazine. Trump finds it safer to be disliked for things he does than for who he is, because the latter taps into his deep fear of not belonging. As surely as he is motivated by a quest for getting even, he is also always driven by a need to be loved.

Trump exacts revenge because he wants to feel better after a narcissistic injury, but there is at work here another motivation even more deeply removed from his conscious understanding: a drive to restore or repair the original broken connection from which his vengeance stems. The individual who seeks revenge is unconsciously attempting to maintain ties to the original, ambivalently held caregiver—in Trump's case, his parents, who are the ultimate targets of all his retaliatory efforts. This is evident, for example, in his legendary battles with Rosie O'Donnell, which of course make more sense when they are seen as being less about Rosie than about his mother, and the deep attachment to his mother's breast that's denied because Rosie was the "rejecting object." After she had a heart attack in 2012, Trump tweeted, "Rosie, get better fast. I'm starting to miss you!" No doubt his profession of missing his revenge object was genuine; he enjoys his retaliatory exchanges with O'Donnell, as they enliven him and function unconsciously to sustain his need to stay connected to the Mary Trump of his childhood. Revenge prolongs both the injury and the link—in this case to his mother, through O'Donnell—and is thus never totally successful.

THE DESTRUCTIVE DRIVE IS evident in an overtly less invasive version of Trump's determination to get revenge: his all-too-familiar practice of blaming others for his own mistakes and wrongdoings. We all blame others at times; it's part of human nature. But Trump's blaming others is instinctive and automatic, seemingly provoked by any perceived criticism. Trump is wired to assign blame so reflexively as to suggest that on a psychological level he is unable to differentiate between pointed but ultimately harmless slights from the NFL or *SNL* and higher-stakes criticisms involving North Korea, Puerto Rico, or China's trade policy.

Blame has its psychological roots in the dynamic, again,

between mother and infant. When the mother disappoints, and the baby responds with what comes to be experienced and identified as anger, the baby thinks it is the mother who is the angry one. Unable to conceive of an explanation for the mother's interrupting her feeding or changing other than her anger, the baby quickly projects his frustration onto the mother, whom he feels is frustrating him on purpose.

When the bond between mother and infant is developing along healthy lines, these disruptions are followed by periods of the mother trying to comfort the baby and restore the broken bond. This process, called "break and repair," gets repeated frequently; each time the mother responds in a reparative fashion, the baby increases his capacity to tolerate frustration, to recognize anger without turning his back on the offending parent. Babies who are not nurtured in this break-and-repair process often grow up to identify themselves as emotionally deprived; not coincidentally, these individuals are less likely to develop frustration tolerance and more likely to blame others for their bad feelings in adulthood.

Trump's reliance on the blaming defense derives from his dynamic with his father as well. Told by Fred Sr. that he must grow up to be a killer and a king, Trump was given the message that constantly maintaining his sense of omnipotence—however misguided—was a prerequisite to receiving his father's approval and avoiding his criticism and rejection. The result has been that Trump has reached a level of defensive grandiosity that would be threatened by any acknowledgment of a mistake.

Unconsciously, Trump never escaped his father: he still lives in fear of his father's disapproval, and in awareness of what happened to Fred Jr. when he failed and incurred his father's disdain and wrath. Trapped in a narcissistic character organization that requires him to deny weakness, Trump maintains his false sense of omnipotence and keeps his father's judgment at bay by blaming others for anything that goes wrong, from failed business ventures like his airline and casinos to his loss of the 2016 popular vote.

Due in part to the narcissistic self-regard he developed in response to his demanding father and unsupportive mother, Donald grew up especially challenged by the prospect of having to accept and internalize those parts of himself that he viewed as unacceptable—particularly anything that suggests weakness, dependency, or other traits that don't fit his omnipotent self-image. We see those parts often projected onto the individuals and institutions to which he assigns blame. Thus his blaming the people of Puerto Rico for depending on others for help is consistent with his inability to recognize the parts of himself that have ever needed help—in infancy or in his career—which he then projects onto Puerto Ricans, on whom he can then inflict the blame and shame he has been programmed to evade since childhood.

The mayor of San Juan made it worse when she pleaded emotionally for his help. Her unfiltered, impassioned entreaty—weeping and begging for help—was all the more threatening to Trump because she was demonstrating the kind of honest, vulnerable admission of need that he can't himself express and must in fact disavow in himself. Once she suggested that he was not being responsive enough, it was predictable, if not inevitable, that he would strike back and accuse her of abandoning her own people. Of course, Trump was the one abandoning his citizens—although the degree to which he fully understands that Puerto Ricans are in fact US citizens remains open to debate.

When Trump did finally try to show up for his presidential duties in hurricane-torn Puerto Rico, his response—tossing paper towels into a crowd of people, who were required to compete with each other to catch them—struck many observers as unbelievably crass. Such observations were in fact on target: a compulsive reliance on the blaming defense does indeed interfere with the individual's capacity for feeling empathy. When a person is as invested in the illusion of his omnipotence as Trump, the capacity to identify with weakness or vulnerability—a requisite for empathy—is too threatening to the delicate balance by which the illusion of omnipotence is maintained. Trump can't admit his own capacity for helplessness at the level that he would need to in order to offer genuine consolation. In the place of empathy, he can offer only contempt for those weaker than him—who embody the weakness that he can't accept in himself. In his eagerness to divert the consequences of his own acts, Trump of course compounds the injury—tossing paper towels instead of repairing Puerto Rico's devastated infrastructure.

While he is unable to project his imperfection or vulnerability onto the unfortunates who are on the receiving end of his own mistakes or assaults, Trump is remarkably adept at the dynamics of projection, which enable him to forge a psychological kinship with other perceived wrongs that have nothing to do with him. In his fall 2017 dust-up with the NFL players who knelt during the national anthem, Trump was apparently taking the protest as a personal insult. At that point he had essentially projected himself into the flag—sadly not surprising for someone whose authoritarian tendencies suggest an identification between the head of state and the state itself that rivals Louis XIV. Trump's disproportionate response—and perhaps willfully inaccurate misreading of the players' protest—befits someone who was feeling victimized because he unconsciously demanded the same respect and reverence he claimed was being denied the flag. His inevitable response was to blame the players—not for their protesting police violence but for a level of anti-patriotism so profound as to lead to a decline in NFL ratings.

By shaming the NFL protesters for their lack of patriotism, Trump engages in the same dynamic of retaliatory projection that he indulges when he references "crooked Hillary." The accusation serves to eviscerate the meaning of the players' actions, separating them from protests against racist police brutality and instead deflecting everything onto himself, as the unconscious embodiment of the American flag. His disparagement overtly serves to distract—but unconsciously declares his own guilt. Blaming is an unconscious confessional; Trump blames others to try to deny an aspect of himself. Whether or not his collusion with Russia is ever established as fact, for example, his refusal to acknowledge and punish Russian meddling in the 2016 election betrays the very anti-patriotism—or treason, in his critique of Democrats who didn't applaud and stand during his 2018 State of the Union Address—that he blames others for displaying.

His blaming others also provides a blueprint for his own future behavior. When as a candidate he was attacking Hillary for risking state secrets, he was outlining his own relationship with Russia; when he accuses Obama and other former presidents of making bad deals, he's predicting future bad deals of his own.

Unfortunately, the stance of omnipotent narcissism from which Trump casts his blame suggests that there will be more bad deals in the future. Because of this long-standing need to evade feeling vulnerable, Trump is easily fooled and manipulated; if he must always be right—because he fears seeming unsure—he needn't think about specifics when making a deal. He ends up with no idea if he is being manipulated. He is so busy avoiding vulnerability or the appearance of weakness that he strikes back instead of thinking. That leaves him in a position where he is less likely to negotiate with the steady, considered discipline that we associate with Obama—or to resist the manipulative overtures of a foreign power seeking to meddle in our elections or our democracy.

The ultimate bad Trump deal may turn out to be his

biggest to date—the deal he made with the voters who elected him president. Before his first year ended, he was clearly failing to uphold his end of the bargain—refusing to defend the country against the Russian threat to its democracy, for example. And he had unleashed his destructive impulse on the constituents who voted for him, jeopardizing their health care and depriving the middle class of promised tax breaks that will instead transfer an immense amount of wealth from the majority of Americans to a tiny fraction of the top 1 percent.

Through it all, he has fomented divisiveness—from within his staff to across the nation as a whole—which is itself a particular kind of expression of the destructive impulse. Divisiveness is a defense practiced by individuals who have serious difficulties managing self-esteem. The divisive individual lacks internal integration—such as the warring aspects of Trump's personality that simultaneously fear and resent his father while also identifying with and emulating him. President Trump must externalize his deep endless conflict, causing unease and ultimately division among others. The divisive individual is himself held captive by his internal split, trapped in a desperate need to fend off despair by continuing to live in some form or other of conflict. He is so in thrall to his destructive impulse that he can't face the prospect of integrating his internal split, which would require facing his own destructiveness. The drive to divide is the drive to oppose integration, first internally and then materially.

The unconscious drive to divide is thus seen as operative in much vaster terms. Trump must hide his lack of internal cohesiveness from himself by attacking the cohesiveness of others, breaking up links between people because he has no solid links internally. The lack of a cohesive self causes him such great envy and anxiety that his setting one group of supporters against another is actually a source of relief. This is a core process that Trump desperately needs to pursue, and something that he will likely chase forever.

In fact, the destructive impulse is rarely if ever satisfied for very long, and as the drive to engage in destructive behavior becomes addictive and grows ever harder to curb, the individual must identify and pursue ever-larger targets. Trump's drive to destroy has already directly targeted Obama's legislative legacy, and his relentless divisiveness can be seen as an attack on Obama as well; by disconnecting Obama's accomplishments from his message of unity, Trump is expressing a seemingly uncontrollable drive to attack his predecessor.

Unfortunately, of course, to attack Obama's legacy of unity is to attack America itself, dividing the nation's people against one another. Trump's indulgence of his destructive and divisive impulses, sourced in the unconscious need to destroy the legacy of his builder-father, are escalating at a rate that suggests he is possibly motivated by an unconscious drive to destroy America by dis-uniting the United States.

Perhaps the destruction is simply a necessary precondition to rebuilding America and making it great again. But Trump is more than likely driven by destruction as an end unto itself.

The forms this destruction might take include war with North Korea or Iran, increased climate vulnerability, deeper divisiveness, trade wars, and more. Once the destructive impulse begins to become felt as a kind of addiction, its most predictable characteristic is escalation, unless or until someone or something intervenes. Failure to intervene places the nation's people, rights, and institutions at increasing risk of ending up as collateral damage in the wake of the externalization of Trump's epic internal struggle.

Chapter Eight

THE PSYCHOLOGY
OF RACISM

A life isn't significant except for its effect on other lives.

— *Jackie Robinson*

I'll say this about one of us living in an all-white suburb:
crabgrass isn't our biggest problem.

—*Dick Gregory*

I am the least racist person you have ever interviewed." So
said Donald Trump to reporters after word got out that
he had referred to African and Caribbean nations as "shithole
countries" and lamented that more immigrants didn't come to
the US from countries "like Norway." Within two months, an
AP poll revealed just how unconvincing Trump's denial had
been, reporting that 57 percent of Americans believed him to
be racist, despite his protestations. His denials after the
"shithole" incident were widely enough reported that a good
portion of that majority believed not only that Trump is a

racist but that he lied—and felt compelled to lie—about it too. Even as Trump's denials go, his "least racist" claim was especially audacious.

The Trump campaign officially began with an unapologetic and categorical denunciation of Mexicans, which was clearly designed to resonate with voters who felt similarly. His first serious test of the presidential campaign waters arguably began with his spearheading the birther movement challenging Obama's citizenship. Although it was widely criticized for its racist intent and appeal, and was the catalyst for Trump's unprecedented public humiliation at the 2011 White House Correspondents Association dinner, Trump's birther campaign— and by extension his racism in general—has in some respects been affirmed by his receiving the ultimate reward, the presidency of the United States.

Though he felt compelled to lie about it, Trump has a history of racism and experiences such impulses on a deep psychological level as having enormous power. Racism also connects him to his personal history and to a generational legacy of bigotry that has characterized the Trump family's approach to business and the world. These attitudes clearly connect him to his supporters as well. As we'll see, the nature of the racist mindset provides some very specific outlines of complex dynamics between the individual and both his inner and outer worlds. What emerges when we look at racism from a psychoanalytic perspective—both in general and Trump's in particular—is that Trump uses racism not simply as a weapon but as an offensive defense, if you will, defending against his own terror that he is, at his core, a compromised human being.

From a psychoanalytic perspective, racism is best understood as an attitude toward people whom the individual considers or experiences as different, or "other." The racist position is dominated by the defense mechanism we know as projection, in which the individual externalizes unwanted characteristics about the self and perceives them in others—or in groups of others that are experienced as being different—whose difference catalyzes a range of irrational fears and obsessions about otherness and dangerous unknowns. When these fears and doubts make the individual feel insecure, and he can project his self-doubts and self-hatred onto a group of others, his insecurity is assuaged; he feels more secure by remaining loyal to his own particular group, and hating and fearing others. The "otherness" of the targeted groups makes it easier to dehumanize them, allowing the racist an avenue to express his hatred—hatred that most likely has its roots in his family of origin. Thus it is safer to express hatred through racist attacks rather than direct hate at one's primary objects of love—one or both parents.

What we know of the parenting that young Donald received in the Trump household makes it likely that it felt less safe for him to express his vulnerabilities than to disavow them and project his feared weakness onto others. By projecting that weakness onto people of color, young Donald was mirroring the model established by his father, who was arrested in a

Queens KKK melee in 1927, and who in subsequent decades built a real estate empire that had been well known in Brooklyn and Queens as developments mainly for whites. In fact, decades before "Trump Tower" became identified—through Donald's relentless media engineering and high-end real estate development prowess, legendary folksinger Woody Guthrie, a resident of Fred Trump's all-white Beach Haven complex, excoriated Fred Trump's discriminatory policies in a journal:

> *I suppose that Old Man Trump knows just how much*
> *racial hate*
> > *He stirred up in that bloodpot of human hearts*
> > *When he drawed that color line*
> > *Here at his Beach Haven family project*

Singer-songwriter and activist Ryan Harvey later set these words to music to create the song "Old Man Trump," with an updated lyric, "Beach Haven is Trump's tower / Where no black folks come to roam."

The firm's racist policies got a considerably more high-profile and extended public airing in the early 1970s, soon after Fred Trump brought his son into leadership of the family business. Suddenly an ongoing investigation by the New York City Commission on Human Rights, in which undercover testers tried to rent Trump apartments, became public. The white applicant was offered housing right away, but the black applicant was told nothing was available. The city shut down rentals, and the Justice Department picked up the case, filing suit in 1973 against father and son, accusing them of "refusing to rent and negotiate rentals with blacks." Trump employees stated that they had been instructed to mark rental applications from blacks with the letter C for "colored."

Donald Trump, then twenty-seven, took the lead in defending the family. Under the tutelage of Roy Cohn, the attorney who had formerly worked for Senator Joseph McCarthy in the Communist witch hunts of the 1950s, Donald pushed back hard, countersuing the government and accusing the prosecutor, who was Jewish, of conducting a "Gestapo-like interrogation." The judge summarily rejected Trump's claims. After years of court battles, Donald Trump sought a settlement, agreeing to buy ads in local newspapers assuring the public that his company would not discriminate—a far lesser penalty than he was initially facing.

The entire episode had a profound and lasting impact on the way Donald Trump would conduct his career. From Cohn, he learned the potential rewards of defending against an attack through the counterattack, a strategy that he continues to this day to deploy. And the relatively mild penalty confirmed that any punishment for the racism that was baked into the family organization's policies could be averted through denial, disavowal, and counterattack.

Despite the rough press he endured during that dispute,

Donald Trump waded into numerous racial controversies throughout his career. In 1989, after five teenage boys—four black and one Hispanic—were arrested for raping and beating a young white female investment banker on a jog through Central Park, Trump bought a full-page ad in the *New York Times* urging swift punishment. Although DNA evidence later exonerated the "Central Park Five," Trump continued to enforce his original position.

Around the same time, Trump offered a telling glimpse of the fears that his racism defends. In a 1989 speech, he said, "A well-educated black has a tremendous advantage over a well-educated white in terms of the job market. And I think that sometimes a black may think that they don't really have the advantage, or this or that, but in actuality today, currently, it's a great [sic]. I said on occasion, even about myself, if I were starting off today I would love to be a well-educated black because I really do believe they do have an actual advantage today."

Those who've worked with Trump for many years say he also has a history of making rough, stereotyping comments about racial minorities. John O'Donnell, who was president of Trump Plaza Hotel and Casino in Atlantic City, said Trump blamed blacks for his financial problems. "I've got black accountants at Trump Castle and at Trump Plaza—black guys counting my money!" O'Donnell quoted Trump as saying. "The only kind of people I want counting my money are short guys that wear yarmulkes every day. . . . Laziness is a trait in blacks. It really is; I believe that. It's not anything they can control." Trump has denied making that remark but has also said, "The stuff O'Donnell wrote about me is probably true."

Trump's personal and family histories shed revealing new light on his response to the white supremacists' demonstration in Charlottesville in 2017—his presidency's first call for leadership in response to an emergency crisis caused by an overt act of racism. Following a disingenuous initial attempt to bring the nation together after the protest turned into a deadly confrontation, Trump surprised some observers when he insisted that there were "good people" among the white supremacists whose angry rally instigated the conflict. Political-minded observers interpreted his clearly unscripted defense of the white supremacists as a concession to the more extreme elements of his base. While there were no doubt some political gains to be made from sending his voters the message that they could be "good" racists, the racist he likely and unconsciously had in mind in his impassioned remarks was his father.

Trump's role as torch carrier for his father's racism is complicated; although he is clearly mirroring a mind-set that he witnessed in his father, we can also understand Donald's racism as a defense against his father. An expression of paranoid anxiety, adult racism is often an outgrowth of childhood feelings of helplessness. It can also be a response to narcissistic injuries in childhood—either being mocked or threatened at home. When normal childhood needs often go unmet, they ultimately thwart emotional growth.

The child of a tyrannical father like Fred Trump may

unconsciously wish to attack back. The impulse to attack one's father, however, can cause guilt and fear of punishment—feelings that the undeveloped individual will (again unconsciously) want to shift outside rather than acknowledge and internalize. Similarly, the anger of a middle child who "loses" his mother to a younger sibling may also induce angry feelings that he can't acknowledge and must project externally. To a white child who entertains compensatory or retaliatory fantasies of being powerful, people with dark skin can present ready-made targets for such projections.

All of us have had unacceptable feelings that we've had to consciously ignore. We may have hated the birth of a sibling and wanted to kill him or her—a wish that clearly was so unacceptable we couldn't even tell our parents. As young children we repress such feelings, pushing them deep into our unconscious until we see a person who might be doing what we had once wanted to do—or thought we did do. Both racism and its psychic cousin xenophobia—a fear of foreigners—are at their hearts driven by a fear of the outsider within—the unfamiliar that lurks inside each of us and at times presents itself in dreams and in sudden realizations about other people.

At a fundamental level, racist feelings are part of the mental process children go through as they develop—that of labeling, defining, differentiating self from other—whether it be girls from boys, tall from short, or brown skin from white skin. It's no accident that students are asked to "compare and contrast" in literature and history classes: it's what we learn to do as part

of defining ourselves and the environments in which we live—
or don't live. Sorting out categories helps organize the mind
and gives the person things to think about without having
them spill over into potentially indefinable chaotic emotions.
Over time, however, categories risk becoming substitutes for
thought. They serve as comforting resources of certainty that
help a person manage anxiety about the unknown or undefined.

Certainty is a defense against anxiety. And categories are
defenses against having to think. When I was in third grade, a
playground bully once asked me, "What are you?" When I
said, "American," the questioner repeated, "Yes, but what are
you?" I could have said a boy, but that would have been obvious. So I asked what he meant. "Where did you come from?"
When I said Los Angeles, he said, "No, where are your parents
from?" When I said Chicago, he said what he wanted to know
was where my grandparents were from, and I again said Chicago. Clearly we were getting nowhere. It turned out that
what he really wanted to know was if I was Jewish. When I
said I was, the kid yelled, "Christ killer!" Obviously that upset
me, though I didn't even know what it meant, other than it
sounded bad. I barely knew what being Jewish even meant.

Whatever our categories are based on, we need them to
sort things out, sometimes in extreme ways. Children need internal absolutes to help them order their minds, before they
tackle the complexity of feeling both love and hate toward the
same person. But some people age into adulthood without
ever learning how to handle that much complexity; racism

offers these adults an opportunity to hold on to those primitive divisions in order to defend against anxiety that might become emotionally paralyzing.

Even if the division is not absolute, the racist individual unconsciously requires the creation and maintenance of an "other" to contain disavowed elements of the self. Racism demands that these projective mechanisms operate continually, keeping the unwanted parts of the self close by, an ever-present reminder to the racist of who he is not. Projection also deprives the self of the possibility to recognize and think about those unwanted internal elements. Instead of looking within, the individual focuses on the recipients of his projections and imagines them as creatively devising new ways to attack, which only further exacerbates the debilitating effects of excessive projection.

Successful projection leaves the racist confident that he is a righteous person, his self-hate transformed into object-hate. He can openly express contempt without guilt, as well as push otherwise painful, narcissistic wounds into people of a different color or nationality. Projection helps one manage anxiety by externalizing onto others what were once experienced as internal threats—unacceptable character traits or emotions including murderousness, delinquency, perversions, and fears of shame, helplessness, or impotence. It results often in blaming or fearing. A liar, for instance, suddenly experiences other people as lying, or a destructive person fears other people as dangerous. Fears of parents can also be displaced onto other authority figures, such as the government or police officers.

Everyone has internal "hooks" on which to hang the unconsciously rejected parts of the self that require projection—dependency, envy, narcissistic injury, castration anxiety, and even hatred. For example, we often see that white people assume that people of color must have menial jobs. When African American reporter April Ryan asked President Trump at a February 2017 press conference about when he would meet with the Congressional Black Caucus, he memorably asked her to schedule a meeting for him. The exchange deservedly raised red flags for its unvarnished glimpse of Trump's racism and sexism; not only had he made the assumption that the CBC members were "friends of [hers]"—betraying the dehumanizing oversimplification of the "other" that makes racism possible—but he had projected onto her the menial role of arranging meetings, an early sign that he would consider meeting with black leaders of Congress as something beneath him. The sexism involved in his assumption about who does scheduling is also palpable. At a deeper level, Trump was likely projecting his own childhood menial roles of picking up after his father on construction sites. For Trump, less than a month in office at the time, the prospect of serving or answering to African American constituents was likely an aspect of his new presidential self that he could not embrace.

Racism was of course at the heart of the speech with which he launched his campaign. Also at its heart were his promises to keep America free from immigrants who had brown skin and spoke Spanish. Tapping into the fears of his followers, he proposed the Mexican border wall, which was a concrete symbol of his deep unconscious need to keep diversity out of his brain as much as out of America. In Trump's psyche, Latin Americans need to be kept separate to protect him from internal conflict that might challenge his self-esteem. Having a split worldview helps him guarantee that he won't have to think about complexity and will be free simply to react as a way to manage his anxiety. Letting in unfamiliar ideas is exceedingly dangerous to him; the promise of building a wall along the Mexican border is really an externalization of a deeply powerful internal need—to keep his father out, or to block out any potential danger, so it never emanates from within.

Trump's unintegrated split worldview helps him maintain a simplified perspective that is a psychological requisite for racist thinking. Another simplification tool is the mind's ability to equate a part with the whole when assessing another person. Racists are able to see only the part of the individual they fear or dislike, rather than seeing the "other" as a whole person or as a member of a group of complex, real people. Racism—like sexism, homophobia, xenophobia, and other kinds of biases—depends upon the individual defining an entire person by a single attribute. A similar kind of thinking informs—or at least infuses—the "lock her up" attacks on Hillary Clinton: her email practices have come to define her among a lot of her opponents, who can more easily demonize and dehumanize her by psychically substituting that part for the whole.

Trump's racism can be detected in his sadistic use of

nicknames, even when they are not overtly racist, as they reveal his comfort at destroying an entire person by mocking one trait. Calling Jeb Bush "low energy" created a label that nobody forgets, like "Mexican rapists" or "lazy" blacks. His ability to generalize, whether about one person or an entire group, reminds us that his capacity to use the part for the whole is essential to his comfort with racism. As a psychoanalyst I try not to diagnose my patients—though insurance forms demand it—because using labels restricts my clinical openness and diminishes my abilities to experience each person individually.

Once the racist individual starts simplifying his thinking in this fashion, some predictable consequences can be expected. The racist resists information that doesn't fit the narrow set of beliefs and assumptions he has embraced, any challenge to which is taken as something to be annihilated or eliminated; the humanity of the immigrant whose family is split up by Immigration and Customs Enforcement (ICE), for example, can thus be overlooked so the racist feels no pain associated with the recognizable heartbreak that ensues. Over time, defining whole groups of people as "others" who are equated with their single damning characteristic restricts the racist's ability to think, feel empathy, or face anxiety—all challenges that Trump appears to be facing unsuccessfully in his presidency.

To the racist, the survival of the self depends on the elimination of the place for shared humanity. Psychoanalytically, it is clear that the more we project and hold firm our beliefs, the less room there is for thought. By defining the "other," the racist not only projects and defines "not me," but also sinks the "other" without a trace, without needing to give that particular group any additional thought. In that respect, racism is a social version of that very human wish not to have to think. Thus we see Donald Trump evacuating his disavowed feelings rather than having to recognize and examine them, because to do so would risk creating room for certainty-threatening doubt.

Unexamined feelings resist evacuation, however, and the racist is left with the emotion at the heart of racism—hate. Deep, passionate emotions drive racist behaviors and sensibilities, and the most pervasive and powerful of these is hatred. It's hard to discover one's own hatred, let alone accept it; it's much easier to see hatred in others, particularly in other groups. But hatred is very powerful and real, and anyone who questions whether it is a driving force in Trump's racism needs only look for it, especially in front of a rally audience. To see Trump almost insisting that team owners fire their kneeling NFL players, for example, is to see the adult version of the toddler throwing rocks at a neighbor in a playpen. Hate must be called by its name, for it is an impediment to any hope for understanding, discussion, or self-reflection.

Hatred is magnified when racism expands from the individual to the group level. Groups are notorious for offering individuals a collective opportunity to escape the restraints imposed by superego or conscience, conferring a shared identity—or "we-ness"—that facilitates expressions of hate and violence more extreme than individuals might feel comfortably committing on their own. That group hate then gets re-introjected by individuals who can act out their violent fantasies and impulses with more impunity, because they have an internal source of support in the form of identification with the group.

As toxic and debilitating as Trump's racism is on an individual, it is even more damaging when he exports it to forge connections with and among his followers. Trump is masterful at manipulating their racist feelings to induce their coming together in their shared projections and hatred. Football star Michael Bennett, in *Things That Make White People Uncomfortable*, wrote that Trump's speech at an Alabama rally "attacked us for protesting and went after the NFL for not firing us. He also described any player who took a knee as a 'son of a bitch.'" Suggesting at times that he can see in his followers the conscious or unconscious memories of childhood traumas like his own, Trump is uncannily effective at activating racist responses to the wounds—real and imagined—that they have in common, and at surfacing memories of racist influences from their pasts. Trump uses his speeches to cut through repression and grab people by their fantasies, without their permission. While memory is fundamental to belonging to history, society, and to one's family, it's also important not to have one's face rubbed in those memories against one's will.

Trump understands racists' instinctive needs to stay in

their own identity group—white, bitter, resentful—and then promotes those needs to his own advantage. In his campaign, Trump was able to generalize and share the experience of outrage at being forgotten, as well as the fury his supporters felt when black and brown men and women—both American citizens and aspiring immigrants—seemed to be encouraged to cut in front of the line, whatever that line was. Thanks to Twitter, Trump is able to export his inner chaos and rage—his racism—with unprecedented speed and reach. For example, when he re-tweeted in the wake of the Charlottesville tragedy an animation of a train smashing into a CNN logo, he not only revealed his petty rage but also offered a glimpse of his own unconscious wish to excuse and even embrace the Charlottesville killer's method of murder by vehicle. For a moment, he betrayed his excitement at running people down as a method of killing—something he previewed by his childlike glee at sitting behind the wheel in big rigs and fire trucks. Having a big engine at his disposal increases his bravery and feelings of potency, as well as the kind of anonymity afforded by road rage.

The way Trump expresses his racism is both consistent and consistently jarring. When he says or tweets some unfiltered appeal to the racist impulses of his followers, it knocks people loose from their underpinnings of reason, conscience, and self-control, and undermines expectations that are part of normal life. Psychoanalysis has given the term "average expectable environment" to the predictable elements of daily life that are so ingrained that they are part of everyone's psyche. We require predictable expectations to help us get through the day and manage the various challenges in our lives. Trump gets through his day, however, by throwing others off balance, in a way that induces his followers to reach out to him to restore their equilibrium.

His claims of "very stable genius" notwithstanding, Trump may strike the disapproving observer—including a majority of American voters—as an unlikely source of stability. By uniting his supporters in a shared projection of opposition to a reviled other, and reuniting them with the lifelong impulses that can give free expression to their racist impulses, Trump is creating a new "average expectable environment" among his supporters that is unacceptable and even threatening to those who don't share it. Trump appeals to his base's collective impulse to define and dehumanize an opposing group as the "other," whether the otherness is defined by difference of race, nationality, or simply difference of beliefs. He offers them the chance to come together against a common foe and feel better about themselves for doing so. In this respect, the psychodynamics behind his and others' racism represent an even bigger threat. Hate begets hate, whether the object of that hatred is people who look different or people who simply think different.

Chapter Nine

THE PSYCHOLOGY OF SEXISM AND MISOGYNY

A woman is a sometime thing.

—Ira Gershwin

Women are raped at levels that have never been seen before.

—President Donald J. Trump

As he tells it, no one respects women more than Donald Trump. He has boasted that the dangers he faced in his years of being sexually active were comparable to the perils of military combat. He said his mother was one of the great people of the world, perhaps the greatest ever. And as a celebrity he bragged that he could get away with grabbing women by the pussy.

Donald Trump's degrading comments and actions toward women are as well documented as his insistence that he treats them with nothing but admiration and respect. Both cannot be true. In that regard, Trump's record with women offers further evidence of several now-familiar aspects of his personality, from narcissism and grandiosity to contempt, pathological lies, and delusions of omnipotence.

As the Trump presidency proceeded into its second year plagued by claims of collusion with Russian election meddlers, he remained haunted by allegations that Russia had compromised him with a video record of a salacious encounter with Moscow prostitutes. The Steele dossier, in which this lurid scenario was laid out, remained neither disproven nor fully corroborated well into 2018. But it rang too true in the context of what was known about Trump's history with women—as well as about his obsessive and vindictive rivalry with Obama, whose preceding Trump in the bed defiled by the Russian prostitutes figures prominently in the story—to be rejected out of hand. If the tale of Trump and the Moscow whores turns out to be fiction, whoever came up with it did his or her research into Trump's psyche.

The ways in which an individual defines and denies his sexuality involve some of the most powerful and complicated impulses that shape the personality. Donald Trump has in the past demonstrated some level of awareness that his physical and internal sex life can be seen as venturing outside what is considered the norm: he has said that his pursuit of women is the one indulgence that he has allowed himself, and he has acknowledged that the way he has spoken about women as a private citizen could be a liability if he ever entered politics.

Upon a closer look, we see that Trump's attitudes toward women offer a window into areas of his psyche that rank among the darkest and most delusional—and perhaps the most determinative.

Donald Trump is a sexist. There is no question that he lusts after women and places high value on their physical appearance. They exist for him as conquests that affirm his power and sexual prowess, or as beautiful sexual companions he uses to incite envy in other men. His sexism is his dehumanization of his women, turning them into functions—the way he did his mother by calling her a "perfect housewife," without describing any of her human qualities.

At its core, sexism is a defensive means of coping with anxiety stemming from a deep fear of the opposite sex, particularly men's fear of women. Rather than confront their fears directly, sexists see themselves as victims of women—consciously or unconsciously. Sexist responses are generally compensatory feelings developed in response to narcissistic injuries, often experienced in childhood and usually rooted in shame and fear. During the first months of life outside the womb, the baby craves that "harmonious mix-up" with the mother or primary caretaker. It is during this quality time that the baby can be completely calmed after being hungry or cold, as mother and baby become one in an all-encompassing connection. It is the loosening of this connection that is essential for the child's independent growth and development. But even after the connection is loosened, unconscious memories of the state of total bliss can endure into adulthood—and provide a lasting sense of connection and confidence.

From what we know of Mary Trump as a maternal figure, we can speculate that this kind of bliss was not something Donald experienced as a baby; in observing him as an adult, it's hard to imagine that he has emotionally intimate relationships.

As babies develop, the mother-infant dynamic shifts, and the child starts wanting to be self-reliant. At this stage, parental help is viewed as weakness, even a source of shame. This is especially true in authoritarian families, in which compassionate or thoughtful men may be demeaned as being weak or indecisive. Young troublemaker Donald Trump's precocious independence likely developed from a premature self-reliant streak, perhaps compensating for feeling mocked or humiliated by not having his mother's loving attention. The adult who never works through these childhood fears of shame will externalize them by shaming others—particularly women who unconsciously remind him of the mother who neglected his needs.

A sexist mind-set and its attendant behaviors are also often seen in men who feel their mothers, older sisters, and teachers victimized them as children. The perception of victimhood—conscious or not—removes any conflict about being destructive to others, which protects against feeling remorse for any future behavior. Although Donald Trump never speaks of his childhood in those terms, the victim dynamic is certainly central to his adult worldview. He positioned himself as the innocent victim of the women who accused him of sexual misconduct. And his charges that he is the target of a partisan witch hunt have grown progressively more frequent and shrill as special prosecutor Robert Mueller's investigation has gotten closer to the White House.

In Trump's use, "witch hunt" is a term fraught with unconscious meaning. The evocation of the twentieth-century witch hunt, masterminded by his mentor Roy Cohn, who schooled Trump in the victim counterstrategy in the 1970s, offers an unintentional glimpse of just how threatened Trump feels. Given his attitudes toward women, Trump adds unconscious new layers into the discussion by bringing witches into it. The victims of the original seventeenth-century witch hunt with whom he is attempting to identify were innocent young girls— an audacious reach, even for Trump. But the very concept of witches has of course long served to contain male anxiety about female power—a pervasive fear that animates Trump's attitudes toward women.

In another astonishingly unguarded passage that helps explain why Trump's 1997 book, *The Art of the Comeback*, is no longer in print, he gives readers a candid glimpse at his thinking.

"Women have one of the great acts of all time," he writes. "The smart ones act very feminine and needy, but inside they are real killers. The person who came up with the expression 'the weaker sex' was either very naive or had to be kidding. I have seen women manipulate men with just a twitch of their eye—or perhaps another body part. I have seen some of the roughest, toughest guys on earth, guys who rant and rave at other tough guys and make them cry, and yet they're afraid of their 120-pound girlfriends or wives."

Trump implies elsewhere that if women behaved like his mother—a wonderful homemaker who took care of his father—they wouldn't be so scary. But those statements mask his deep frustration with her, and of the power her dismissiveness had over him. As he grew older, he writes elsewhere in *The Art of the Comeback*, "and witnessed life firsthand from a front-row seat at the great clubs, social events, and parties of the world . . . I began to realize the women are far stronger than men." While he insists that there is "nothing I love more than women . . . they're really a lot different than portrayed. They are far worse than men, far more aggressive, and boy, can they be smart. Let's give credit where credit is due, and let's salute women for their tremendous power, which most men are afraid to admit they have."

Passages like these offer a reminder of why psychoanalysis has long associated the male fear of female power with castration anxiety. Trump's remarkably direct acknowledgment that he is threatened by female power is a textbook illustration of a man who fears being emasculated by a woman. Castration anxiety has been discussed ever since Freudian psychoanalysis burst on the scene before World War I. Based on the myth of Oedipus, who was punished for sexually desiring his mother, castration anxiety posits that women hold a mysterious power over men that can rob them of their agency. Castration anxiety is frequently at the heart of what are experienced as sexist attitudes, but can also be seen as fears of the unknown otherness of women as described by Trump.

Trump unconsciously demonstrated his own considerable castration anxiety throughout the 2016 campaign against Hillary Clinton—the "nasty woman" whose power was so threatening to him that he wanted to lock her up. At the same time, he tried to sow doubt about her power, questioning her stamina and even her health. In these instances he was expressing his particular antipathy toward older women—Clinton, Nancy Pelosi, Elizabeth Warren—who grow more threatening as they age past the relative youth of young Oedipus's mother and accrue power and independence that expand far beyond the bounds of motherhood.

In this way, Trump is both acting upon and activating in others the deepest of all pathologies: the primitive hatred of the mother, in response to what is experienced as rejection when she progresses beyond the focus on her baby that comes with new motherhood. As much as Trump overtly idealizes his mother when he has spoken or written about her, his more common attitude of demeaning women feels like an inversion of that idealization. Trump unconsciously displaces onto other women the resentment toward his mother that is too painful to confront and accept.

This hostility is often directed at other mothers, or at the institutions of motherhood and family. With immigration policies that forcibly separate mothers from children, for example, Trump is tapping into deeply primitive fantasies in his followers that involve breaking up the family. Trump's comfort with breaking up families is reminiscent of an attitude that I've seen develop among certain fathers, particularly those who felt unloved by their own mothers. When their wives become mothers, those fathers begin unconsciously to envy their own children who were suddenly having a better mother than they ever had themselves. For someone as envious of other people's well-being as Trump, the prospect of spoiling what is good in another family has a powerful and unconscious appeal.

It was reported in 2018 that Trump went to the CIA and watched footage of "a previously recorded strike in which the agency held off on firing until the target had wandered away from a house with his family inside. Trump asked, 'Why did you wait?'" And sometimes the hostility toward family is directed at targets closer to home, such as when he bent over for a porn star to spank him with a magazine that featured his family's photo on the cover.

Trump's sexist attitudes are more frequently expressed in the insults and degrading comments that he regularly directs at a wide range of women. Many of these remarks are focused on women's appearance, and betray an astonishingly juvenile character. Rosie O'Donnell was publicly labeled "disgusting, both inside and out" with a "fat, ugly face." Former Miss Universe Alicia Machado was also labeled "disgusting," as well as

"Miss Piggy," for having gained weight. Viewers of one of the 2016 Republican primary debates were invited to "look at that face," when he was demeaning fellow candidate Carly Fiorina. "Would anyone vote for that? Can you imagine that, the face of our next president?"

Implicit in the tone of his insults is the defiant suggestion that he won't grow up. Like a potty-mouthed child who seeks attention by talking dirty, Trump indulges in locker-room language when insulting women as a rebuke to his mother. Defiantly asserting that he won't grow up, he is still punishing his mother for having another son after him, for desiring his father, or for remaining distant as young Donald demonstrated that he was not maturing like a normal, healthy child.

Some of Trump's highest-profile insults toward women suggest a direct unconscious connection with the difficult circumstances of his younger brother's birth. Megyn Kelly famously had "blood coming out of her whatever," a vivid evocation of Mary Trump's near-fatal postpartum hemorrhaging. Mika Brzezinski was also bleeding—in Trump's telling, from a "really bad face-lift," which speaks to Trump's resentment that women are so selfish as to age beyond their traditional prime child-bearing years, despite the false claim's origins in Trump's fevered imagination. Megyn, Mika, Mary—mother—all of them blond, all of them rejecting Donald, at least in his primitive perception.

In Trump's view, otherwise powerful women deserve degradation if in his estimation they reflect badly on men. A pair of 2015 tweets asked, "If Hillary Clinton can't satisfy her husband, what makes her think she can satisfy America?" and "How much money is the extremely unattractive (both inside and out) Arianna Huffington paying her poor ex-hubby for the use of his name?" His anti-Huffington quip applies to many other women whose looks he's maligned over the years.

By placing so much value on women's appearance, and declaring their potential to make men look better or worse, Trump is unconsciously acknowledging how much power he gives them in his way of thinking. He fears ceding that much power, and attacking women verbally is a way to restore power to himself. In psychoanalysis, this kind of behavior is considered "counter-phobic"—meaning, an action that is unconsciously motivated to defend against fear. While aware of women's power over men, Trump regularly behaves as if women are not dangerous. He feels consciously brave, because he's a wealthy celebrity, free to grab whenever he wants. (Perhaps I am counter-phobic in writing this book, since half the world—and all of the Republican Party—seems so frightened of scrutinizing this emperor and looking beneath his new clothes.) Another fear that Trump projects onto women is that they will leave him—again, like his mother did, at least in his understanding—which he addresses by demanding total loyalty from the women in his life. "Loyalty is everything to me," he told Nancy Collins in 1994. "I'm completely loyal, I don't understand disloyalty—why my father couldn't understand why I would leave Ivana."

In the same interview, he revealed some of the terms of

what he considered wifely loyalty—which he felt his ex-wife, Ivana, had violated by going to work at one of his casinos. "I don't want to sound like a chauvinist, but when I come home at night and dinner's not ready I go through the roof," he explained. "But I got handed casino numbers. After twelve hours dealing with my companies, I didn't want to talk business. I can instantaneously shut it off, my survival mechanism. But she'd be yelling into the phone at the casino; I didn't want my wife shouting like that. Ivana had a great softness that disappeared. She became an executive, not a wife."

At an unconscious level—the level I work with in my consulting room—Trump is saying his wife must subordinate her needs to his, or risk the consequences. While heightened by the particulars of his early childhood, the psychological premium that Trump places on loyalty when it comes to the women in his life can be traced to a near-universal yearning for that state of total bliss of the earliest mother-infant dynamic. For young Donald that bliss was short-lived, and he now demonstrates an infant's greed for total loyalty and complete attention from those tasked with meeting his needs.

In extreme cases, the adult individual craves an even earlier blissful circumstance, and can be seen attempting to re-create the safety and isolation of the womb. Prior to the White House, Trump secluded himself in the gilded haven of his Trump Tower apartment, whose glittering gold surfaces evoke Mary Trump's affinity for luxury. Trump's unusual request for an extra lock on his White House bedroom door—for which security would not have a key—suggests that he is again trying to create a private retreat in which he can feel psychologically safe, nestled in womb-like isolation. None of these ploys works for him, though, because the only real way for him to evolve is to face his rage at his mother, mourn what he never got from her, and move on.

Instead, we were reminded in the winter of 2018, he pursues a legislated loyalty, imposing nondisclosure agreements on women who might be in a position to betray him. It is not coincidental that the affairs Stormy Daniels and Karen McDougal fought to make public both began soon after Trump's third wife, Melania, gave birth to their son, Barron. On the wounded-child level, Melania's becoming a mother was experienced as an act of disloyalty by Trump—he had once again lost the main source of his replacement for maternal attention to a baby boy. Trump tipped his unconscious hand by naming his son Barron, the name that Trump formerly used when he assumed a fake identity, which also evoked the name of the Hilton heir who Trump contemptuously dismissed as a member of the "Lucky Sperm Club." The name choice suggests that Trump unconsciously recognized his resentment at baby Barron for usurping his place at Melania's breast—enough for Donald to feel entitled to pursue a replacement outside the marriage. At the same time, he was still worried enough about maternal retribution that he would pay off Daniels and McDougal to keep silent.

One detail he likely hoped to keep silent involved his daughter Ivanka. Trump reportedly told both Karen McDougal and Stormy Daniels in their initial encounters that they reminded him of his beautiful older daughter. Why would a man about to cheat on his wife talk about his beautiful daughter? Ivanka, who was twenty-four at the time, was in LA to costar with her father on the sixth season of *The Apprentice*. I think that Trump's likening those two women to Ivanka served two purposes: he could enact an unconscious incestuous fantasy without feeling guilt—after all, he wasn't having sex with his daughter; and he thought he could perform better by using the image of Ivanka as a kind of psychological Viagra. A father's incestuous wishes, which are not uncommon, are partly driven by unconscious narcissistic feelings that his daughter has half of his genes, allowing him to unconsciously imagine having sex with the most beautiful part of himself. At the same time, by superimposing Ivanka onto other women, Trump unconsciously tries to protect her from the danger that he might act on his incestuous urges. We've all seen pictures of the hungry way he has looked at her over the years. At the GOP convention we saw Trump slide his right hand down Ivanka's bare arm onto her buttocks, forcing her artfully to turn away from him. And most recently, those who watched Playboy Playmate Karen McDougal's interview with Anderson Cooper saw a "family" picture with Melania on one end and Karen McDougal on the other—and Ivanka next to her father with their bodies turned into each other, chest to chest as the picture's focal point. Barely visible was Trump's left hand, again on his daughter's behind.

This grandiose narcissism that violates a daughter's expectable boundaries ultimately dehumanizes her, consciously violating her and unconsciously changing her from human daughter to nonhuman property. Women and his family name are all part of the Trump brand, his property.

Such intense fantasies, even if not acted on, also unconsciously attack the family structure. While Trump's affair with McDougal protected both Ivanka and himself, it assaulted his newly formed three-person family—himself, Melania, and baby Barron.

By purchasing his mistresses' silence, Trump also reminds us of the continued ease with which he treats women like property. This is perhaps never clearer than in his buying, owning, and selling beauty pageants, which celebrate the objectification of their female contestants. Trump made it clear what he felt that ownership entitled him to when boasting to Howard Stern of walking into the Miss Universe dressing room whenever he wanted to. "I'm allowed to go in, because I'm the owner of the pageant and therefore I'm inspecting it," he told Stern. Reducing "these incredible-looking women" to an *it* to be inspected offers a sadly predictable progression along the spectrum of dehumanization that characterizes so many of Trump's actions. Still, on some level he recognizes the essential wrongness of what he's doing, telling Stern that he is able to "sort of get away with things like that" because of his ownership of the pageant—much like he was able to get away with assaulting women, boasting on the infamous *Access Hollywood* tape that this was a benefit of his celebrity.

Getting away with it is a big part of what drives Trump's abusive treatment of women. He has good reason to think that his efforts are successful: after all, he was elected president despite multiple allegations of sexual assault and misconduct. Trump's relationships and interactions with women provide him an opportunity to act upon the delusions of omnipotence that are fed every time he gets away with something else. As we have seen, Trump's fragile sense of self is dependent upon his feeding those delusions—so much so that one might rightfully wonder what will serve as a psychic replacement for his sexual behavior when his actions are curtailed by the restrictions of the presidency.

Meanwhile, Donald Trump indirectly expresses his hatred of women when he turns a blind eye to men accused of abusing women. For years he's said that most men accused of abuse were actually reacting to having been wronged by women. He has knowingly hired or supported enough abusers or pedophiles to suggest a pattern: White House secretary Rob Porter, speechwriter David Sorensen, adviser Steve Bannon, campaign manager Corey Lewandowski, secretary of labor nominee Andrew Puzder, and Alabama senatorial candidate Roy Moore. Some he explicitly defended, others he merely enabled by looking the other way. Perhaps he credits them with following the philosophy he revealed to *New York* magazine in 1992: "Women: you have to treat 'em like shit."

Violence against women is of course also against the law. Trump's defense of abusive behavior—along with his own flagrantly extramarital affairs—is fueled by his contempt for women, for their rights, and for the laws and institutions that protect them. Trump has repeatedly asserted that laws and norms don't apply to him. His attitudes toward women remind us once again that Trump's delusions of omnipotence include an assumption that he can live above or outside the rule of law.

The antipathy Trump demonstrates toward women doesn't exist in a vacuum. Michael Wolff's *Fire and Fury* makes it clear that Trump's contempt is directed not just at his own marriage and the legal constraints it places on his behavior but on the institution of marriage itself. According to Wolff, "Trump likes to say that one of the things that made life worth living was getting your friends' wives into bed." Wolff describes an elaborate ruse whereby he would trick his male friends into making disparaging comments about their wives and their sex lives while their wives were secretly listening—all in the name of getting the wives to sleep with him. These are the actions of an individual who is driven by contempt for other people's marriages as well as his own.

Ultimately Trump's parents' marriage is also the unconscious focus of his contempt. We see in Trump's philandering a stark illustration of Oedipal displacement; his efforts to get

married women to prefer him over their husbands are unconscious attempts to escape the memory of his mother, who was
dismissive to little Donny and loyal to her husband. By undermining his friends' marriages he is attacking his parents'
union—the one area where, we'll recall, Fred Trump chided
Donald that the father bested the son by never divorcing or
remarrying.

To compensate for his frustrations, Donald tried to bed as
many women as possible—another assertion of his delusion of
omnipotence. Trump characterized his youthful promiscuity
as his "own personal Vietnam," joking that he slept with so
many women that his life was endangered by the possibility of
catching a venereal disease. He also unconsciously revealed
that he regarded his female conquests not as lovers but as
dangerous enemy combatants. Excessive indulgence of one's
own impulses can be seen as a form of narcissistic flirting
with disaster, proving one's omnipotence by testing its limits.
The continuation of affairs into his third marriage, such as the
McDougal and Daniels escapades that he apparently tried to
silence after the fact, suggests that he continued to court disaster with the confidence that his wealth and power could
protect him from any significant recourse.

Women, wives, mistresses, and even daughters are turned
into objects used for a ritual competition Trump is unconsciously waging against his father, whom he can never defeat—
as Fred once told him. He plays his dehumanizing game to
make other men envious and to remind himself that he doesn't

need or desire his mother. In Wolff's telling, men and husbands—even friends—are pulled into this game as well. The disrespect for humanity that is expressed through Trump's misogyny is clearly not limited to the female half of the population; his hatred is easy to see in his generally misanthropic worldview. He willfully put immigration policies in place so he could break up families through deportation—actions that are unconsciously linked to his own families. Trump's misogyny and misanthropy are already palpable, and the potential for continued damage is staggering to contemplate.

Chapter Ten

THE LANGUAGE OF DONALD TRUMP

Don't do what I say; do what *I* say.

—*W. C. Fields*

All of the true things I'm about to tell you
are shameless lies.

—*Kurt Vonnegut*

In the opening lines of *Trump: The Art of the Deal*, the 1987 bestseller that launched Donald Trump as a national figure, Trump invites his readers to believe that his life as a deal maker is motivated not by commerce, but by art. "I don't do it for the money," he writes. "Deals are my art form. Other people paint beautifully on canvas or write wonderful poetry. I like making deals, preferably big deals."

As hard to believe as they may now be, these claims with which Trump sought to introduce himself to a mass audience began outlining the master negotiator persona that millions of Americans thought they were voting for when they elected him

TRUMP ON THE COUCH

president. We should have paid closer attention to what he was saying; later in the same opening chapter, he unconsciously alerted readers that the character he was constructing—the deal maker as an artist—was a fraud.

The revelation, for attentive readers, comes in a scene when he pays an out-of-nowhere morning visit to a "highly successful and very well known painter," who suddenly interrupts their conversation to ask if Trump wants to watch him "earn twenty-five thousand dollars before lunch." The painter then "picked up a large open bucket of paint and splashed some on a piece of canvas stretched on the floor," Trump writes. "Then he picked up another bucket, containing a different color, and splashed some of that on the canvas. He did this four times, and it took him perhaps two minutes. When he was done, he turned to me and said, 'Well, that's it. I've just earned twenty-five thousand dollars. Let's go to lunch.'" The artist's point, Trump writes, was that "collectors wouldn't know the difference between his two-minute art and the paintings he really cares about," an insight he found so striking that he would "sometimes wonder what would happen if collectors knew what I knew about my friend's work that afternoon."

The memory is presented as an aside, a throwaway moment that is never again referred to in the pages that follow. Also thrown away—but forever foregrounded in the title—is the conceit of the deal maker as artist, which never reappears after Trump's opening-lines effort to justify his greed and ambition as being the more respectable attributes of an artistic pursuit.

In fact, the only other artists mentioned in *The Art of the Deal* are the above-mentioned painter who tricks his collectors, con artists, a "bullshit artist," and a purported turnaround artist whom Trump bests in the Trump Tower deal.

In psychoanalysis, openings and asides can often yield disproportionately useful insights; in light of the value Trump places on his deal-making prowess, it's worth considering how his portrait of the artist as a manipulative fraud reverberates throughout the self-portrait that follows. Almost certainly without consciously intending to, Trump is letting his readers know that the word *art* in the title is a ruse, the deals he strikes are likely not what they seem, and the words he uses to make his deals are likely as random as paint splashed on a canvas in the minutes before lunch.

In the years that have followed the publication of *The Art of the Deal*, Trump's deal-making skills and practices have deservedly come under scrutiny—and have often not measured up. It turns out that it's hard to make deals with someone who can't be trusted, or to negotiate with a pathological liar. Trump has demonstrated this on countless occasions as president, but never more explicitly than in a pair of televised bipartisan conferences in which Trump invited Democrats to make deals with him on immigration and gun control. After making a show of publicly advocating progressive new positions during the negotiating sessions, Trump later retreated to his previous stances, scuttling Democrats' hopes of making the deals he had encouraged them to pursue. The surprising new positions were abandoned as quickly as they were articulated; the deal artist's palette, it turned out, included a readiness to make a disingenuous show of appearing to search for a consensus that was less forum than farce, and of a willingness to speak in language disconnected from its apparent meaning or intent.

When language is disconnected from meaning, it serves other psychological functions. Rather than contain or convey meaning, language is used to deflect or distract, to obscure intent or contempt, and to assert power. Language can also be used to carry music, emotional signs and codes that communicate on a nonverbal level. As a psychoanalyst I try to listen to my patients' words but also to their music. For people who listen to words as music, Trump's language is more than simply idiosyncratic: it is the language of a salesman who conveys emotion that serves primarily to call attention to himself. For most of my patients, I think the music is out of their conscious awareness. But President Trump demonstrates a keen awareness of this often-ignored communication tool, and we see that most often in impromptu moments at rallies or unscripted interviews.

Trump's idiosyncratic use of language has prompted linguistic experts to ponder his style, syntax, rhetorical techniques, and even his intelligence. Looking more closely at some of the most pervasive aspects of his use of unscripted language reveals that behind the tortured syntax are symptoms of several worrisome disorders.

On August 15, 2017, Trump spoke with reporters at Trump Tower about his delay in responding to the death of Charlottesville protester Heather Heyer, who was hit by a car driven by a white nationalist:

> *I didn't wait long. I didn't wait long. I didn't wait long. I wanted to make sure, unlike most politicians, that what I said was correct. Not make a quick statement. The statement I made on Saturday, the first statement, was a fine statement. But you don't make statements that direct unless you know the fact. It takes a little while to get the facts. You still don't know the facts. And it's a very, very important process to me. And it's a very important statement. So I don't want to go quickly and just make a statement for the sake of making a political statement. I want to know the facts—*

Trump clearly struggles here to respond coherently to questions that put him—or perhaps the persona he has created—on the spot. First, he repeatedly deflects criticism until he can get to the next thought. (In other instances where feelings of criticism or hostility overwhelm him, his fallback technique is simply to shout "fake news.") Then, attempting to explain his delayed response to Heyer's death, he claims he wanted all the "facts" or "fact." He can't even agree with himself, a complication of the extreme anxiety that makes it nearly impossible to think clearly. Struggling to connect his thoughts, Trump uses a declarative word from one sentence to link it to the next, as when he said "important" before segueing into "important statement." Then he repeats "statement" for the next sentence, before finally returning to the word "facts."

His vagueness is about memory and content, both of which have been compromised by years of marketing himself rather than a product or service that he would have to think or learn about. His response is similar to his assertion that he doesn't have time to watch TV—a demonstrable lie—because he's busy reading "documents," a term as vague as "statement." Trump uses the word *facts* as if he has them, but he can't articulate what those facts are or what they mean.

In an AP interview on the occasion of his first one hundred days as president, Trump addressed a question about the various GOP factions that disagreed over health care:

> *So the Republican Party has various groups, all great people. They're great people. But some are moderate, some are very conservative. The Democrats don't seem to have that nearly as much. You know the Democrats have . . . they don't have that. The Republicans do have that. And I think it's fine. But you know there's a pretty vast area in there. And I have a great relationship with all of them. Now, we have government not closing. I think we'll be in great shape on that. It's going very well. Obviously, that takes precedent.*

Besides the obvious homophone (*precedent* and *president*), this passage conveys a sense of space, vast and great. The lawmakers he references all link back to him and are blurry background characters. His facility at speaking in the vernacular and falsely convincing people that he can fix things is an asset for a real estate agent but a serious problem for the president of the United States. Trump places particular emphasis on the word *great*, in reference to relationships, groups, and individuals. Rarely does Trump use any specific or nuanced adjectives in an impromptu setting, apparently unable to summon the necessary powers of thought and reflection in the anxiety of the moment.

It has memorably been said that the voters considered collectively as President Trump's base take his words seriously but not literally. His opponents, on the other hand, at least initially, did the reverse, taking his words literally without taking them—or Trump—seriously. A psychoanalytic investigation, however, must do both and more; we must take his words both literally and seriously, but also look beyond or beneath their literal meanings to identify unintentional glimpses of the unconscious forces that drive their choice and use.

WORDS, IN PSYCHOANALYSIS, ARE usually the product of thought, which is typically the precursor to action. Trump has the manner of speech of someone for whom the boundaries between words, thoughts, and actions are indistinguishable. He speaks—and tweets—without apparent thought. He simply acts—or, more frequently, reacts. For all his prodigious abilities—making deals, expanding his brand, vanquishing all rivals to get elected president—he lashes out uncontrollably when challenged by a situation that calls upon him to think and speak on his feet.

Trump is often unable to finish sentences, which makes it hard for him to feel that he's "on the same page" with people who do. It's as though Trump actually interrupts his own thinking with a new thought or association that only he can interpret. He circles around his original idea, which is something psychoanalysts call "tangential thinking"—a pattern of speech characterized by oblique, digressive, or irrelevant replies to a question. This is sometimes considered a thought disorder, while other mental health professionals see it as indicative of the manic phase of bipolar illness, or even the result of a dependency on amphetamines.

Beyond tangential thought patterns, President Trump's syntax frequently demonstrates a range of particular and now-familiar characteristics, ranging from dishonest content—lying, inciting polarization or violence, mocking, exaggerated promises, self-reference—to a disjointed style marked by the repetition of phrases, the use of adjectives and adverbs as nouns, and clang associations, which define words and phrases by how they sound, when their actual meaning is unknown to the speaker.

Trump's tendency to repeat key words and phrases is so prevalent that some critics have interpreted it as a sign of cognitive decline—perhaps even early-onset Alzheimer's, which we know from his father's experience runs in the family. There's certainly no reason to rule out cognitive decline, but there's also no denying the effectiveness of this particular verbal tic; Trump's use of repetition, whether just a single adjective like *crooked* for Hillary Clinton or more elaborate falsehoods and accusations, suggests he has an unconscious understanding of the power of repetition to shape perception in others. The reiteration of phrases like "lock her up," "drain the swamp," and "fake news" can be so powerful as to expand upon if not outright replace their literal meaning, with each epithet unleashing a flood of feelings among his listeners.

Trump frequently indulges in the repetition of empty adjectives, like *great, tremendous*, or *smart*—repeating them without in fact investing them with any additional meaning, much like children saying that they "really, really, really" feel or know something because they actually lack more precise words to describe their feelings. Unable to find the words that will specify a richer meaning, he uses and repeats the same hollow adjectives, conveying emotion and power in a way that renders the words themselves meaningless. The repetition likely also reassures him that he is making sense—which he knows enough to know is not a given with him—and that he is coming off as the absolute authority, when in fact he may be trying to convince others of something he himself isn't convinced of.

Trump never seems embarrassed when he has trouble expressing ideas. He simply moves forward, as though unaware of his disability. While language-based learning disabilities can cause some people to devalue themselves, Trump displaces his own debased self-esteem onto others and attacks them rather than risk self-criticism. A case in point were his attacks on Obama for not being able to speak without using a teleprompter—a clear example of projection, and of the delusion that the verbal abilities he could be observed demonstrating on *The Apprentice* were in fact his own rather than the result of a heavily produced television program. In fact, according to *Celebrity Apprentice* contestant Clay Aiken, the producers fed Trump lines through a teleprompter-like device on his desk that was disguised to look like a phone. As for the weekly dismissals, "Trump didn't actually decide when to fire a contestant," Aiken told the *Washington Post*. "He didn't make those decisions, he didn't fire those people."

A close examination of Trump's language begins to identify cracks even in its simplicity. For instance, he often uses words and phrases that mean the opposite of their apparent meaning. After saying he was going to appoint the best and greatest people to his cabinet and to the judiciary, he named cabinet secretaries with little to no experience with—if not antipathy toward—the agencies they were put in charge of, and chose judicial appointees who lack the experience, training, and temperament to fulfill their duty to the public good.

With this in mind, it's worth looking more closely at what

is perhaps his favorite adjective, the aspiration at the heart of his campaign slogan. In Trump's usage, *great* is a wish and a sales tactic more than a fact. The word is so vague as to be meaningless, as in his November 9, 2016, victory speech: "First I want to thank my parents, who are looking down on me right now. Great people . . . They were wonderful in every regard. I had truly great parents." Trump's inability to think of more specific adjectives to describe his parents and the lessons he learned from them speaks both to the lack of intimacy he shared with them as well as his own (not unrelated) narcissism, which extends to the rest of his family as well. "They are great," he said when he thanked his living siblings. "And also my late brother Fred. Great guy, fantastic guy. Fantastic family; I was very lucky. Great brothers, sisters; great unbelievable parents." Anyone who has noticed how rarely Trump has spoken of his living siblings since then will recognize that making America great again will not, from his perspective, mean that he will be required to give much thought to it.

By now it is common among close observers of his use of language to conclude that there is quite possibly something seriously wrong with President Trump. It's useful to name what we've been seeing: it is my opinion that Donald Trump likely suffers from a subtype of dyslexia—a neuropsychological condition that was likely present and undetected since early childhood. It is a subtle language-processing disorder that affects emotional, cognitive, and social development. Traditionally, dyslexia is diagnosed when a child has problems mastering single-word reading as well as spelling and being able to sound out words. A difficulty understanding what someone else is saying, called auditory processing, often accompanies this reading problem. While dyslexia is now more recognized and successfully treated, it remains a chronic condition with life-long ramifications. While it is fundamentally neurological in origin, dyslexia is also affected by the quality of care given the child in his first several years, made more difficult because dyslexic children are often impulse-ridden and easily unsettled, so they require understanding and comforting to help them learn to modulate their own emotions and anxieties. Emotional consequences follow, and may involve lying, exaggerating, and feigning certainty about things they do not comprehend. They feel shame at not knowing, and at having difficulty with reading comprehension. Children with language-processing disorders require attentive parenting to help them manage. Several of Donald Trump's familiar adult personality traits—including his trademark volatility, lack of impulse control, and insistence that he knows better than anyone else—evoke the recognizable hallmarks of an undertreated childhood learning disability.

While dyslexia is commonly understood to refer to the child's limited reading and spelling capabilities, it affects more than intellectual development. It is a problem processing experiences, especially involving language, and the ability to process information in order to think and then express what one has concluded. When a person cannot regulate his feelings, he converts them into action, often impulsive action. A person who cannot self-regulate has trouble sitting still, paying attention, and even making sense of what people are talking about. Five generals reported in early 2018 that President Trump perseverated when they tried to discuss Syria. "What do we get in return for our investment?" he reportedly kept repeating, apparently unable to think about what they were telling him. It's easy to envision young Donny having similar trouble in the classroom listening to his teachers. This difficulty sheds new light on Trump's tale of hitting a second-grade music teacher he found ineffective; the teacher couldn't be effective because Trump didn't understand what was being said, even when he apparently wanted to.

The adult inability to tolerate uncertainty and process thoughts and new ideas into words can often be traced to infancy. Before babies can talk, their actions and emotional expressions are observed and understood as "language" by the mother or primary caretaker. If the baby is agitated and distracted, his preverbal "communication" may be harder for the caregiver to make sense of—and the result would be a less harmonious mix-up between mother and child. The agitated baby in turn does not develop the capacity to overcome his anxiety long enough to think.

Donald Trump has had behavioral problems since early childhood, most of which included impulsive acting out of his feelings; lacking the words or the patience to articulate his feelings, he resorted to excessive physical activity, sometimes violent, often disruptive. This kind of acting out likely com-promised Trump's ability to learn as well as to express him-self verbally, which in turn caused trouble in his ability to comprehend what others say. Language-processing challenges such as these can cause a wide range of problems in children, resulting in impaired abilities to read, write, reason, speak, hold one's temper, and more. What probably began as a neuro-logical deficit quickly became a psychological disorder—as there is no evidence his parents or teachers focused on any-thing other than his disruptive behavior. Underlying anxiet-ies, most likely related to extreme learning disabilities, were seemingly not addressed. As he developed, Trump compen-sated for his inability to think clearly on his feet by learning how to read people—and eventually well enough to success-fully sell something to them.

Trump's patterns as an adult make some who know or ob-serve him question his intelligence. Remarkably, the report that his first secretary of state called him a moron engendered little to no discussion of whether the characterization was ac-curate. Regardless of his innate intelligence, his ability to learn was compromised sufficiently to leave him ignorant about a wide range of topics. Because learning was a struggle, he compensated by developing a grandiose persona. He at-tacked the reality of his limitations with contempt for school-work, which we now see echoed in his contempt for the work of serving in the presidency.

Childhood learning struggles often lead to further challenges in adulthood. People with language-processing trouble often blame others for not being clear, which leads to paranoid thinking. At times they feel like someone is trying to fool them when in fact they just don't understand what's being said. People with this kind of confusion are on an emotional roller coaster of anger and frustration frequently cited by Trump observers; swinging between grandiosity and shame, he struggles to convert feelings into words, unable to develop a consistent sense of self-respect.

Young Donald's untreated hyperactive tendencies set off a vicious circle of problems that continue to escalate. His inability to sit still limited his intellectual development; unfortunately, language development is necessary for developing impulse control, which Trump has in woefully short supply. As his Twitter feed demonstrates, when President Trump feels something, he must express it immediately, with whatever words possible. Trump's tweets present him an appealing medium for evacuating his anxieties without processing or learning from them, which further impedes the intellectual development that might help him bring his impulses under control. On and on it goes, made worse by the confluence of factors that prevent him from fulfilling one of the key psychological duties of the presidency—helping Americans contain their anxieties and manage their fears. Traditionally, presidents have been able to contain their own anxieties in order to help us contain ours; Trump is unable to do so, continuing to prefer tweets to measured thought. Instilling calm is not his strong suit; instead, dominated by his chaotic inner world, he is a prisoner of his own anxiety, which he attempts to manage by inflicting it on the rest of us. Inevitably, our mounting anxiety is mirrored by his own, making matters worse for all involved.

Further aggravating the situation is the personal nature of both the slights Trump feels he experiences and the attacks with which he responds. Dyslexia is often associated with having thin skin, as children confuse questions with criticism or even attack. We are all familiar with times when any critical challenge feels like a personal affront; pride and a little leftover crypto grandiosity are present in all of us. President Trump, however, demonstrates little ability to manage criticism—even when it comes in the form of simple questions asked by the press. Questions make him feel flooded, a feeling he attempts to reverse by flooding us with tweets, changing the subject, and pushing his own uncertainty onto us. He reflexively personalizes questions, transforming his responses into vindictive ad hominem attacks. The complex problems he cannot address inevitably continue to escalate, requiring further attention down the road. The idea of being made, or held, accountable for his actions is his greatest fear of all.

Defenses formed in response to childhood language and learning challenges can take a variety of forms in their efforts to protect against anxiety. Trump discovered that defining the world as dog-eat-dog helped him focus—though it didn't help him read or understand nuance. He compensated in a variety of ways, especially when there is nobody to recognize his cognitive difficulty, let alone help him make sense of his experiences. All that could be done then was to set limits, so Donny learned to compensate by feeling grandiose and certain, and impatiently rushing to act whenever he felt emotionally threatened. Some people prematurely develop advanced social skills, able to read people when they can't read a book. Some become bullies, trying to force their own feelings of shame onto others. Some use certainty as a defense against fears of not knowing. Some only use words with the broadest common definitions. Some use words to obfuscate. Some use words that have many different meanings. Trump increasingly developed grandiose defenses. We see him claim to know "the best words," and to say that he alone "can fix it." Unfortunately, people with language-processing difficulties can't use words to help regulate feelings, which dramatically limits what they're able to fix.

Trump developed other psychological defenses to manage this problem. In addition to bullying and shaming others—forcing his own debased self-esteem onto them—he developed compensatory grandiose fantasies. His grandiose claims of knowing "the best words" play a protective role that helps him maintain his denial of his desperate reliance on nonthought (not to mention a mostly monosyllabic vocabulary). Grandiose proclamations—such as "I alone can fix it"—provide a more comfortable alternative to the threatening challenges of having to think, pay attention, or try to understand.

As a candidate, Trump knew he couldn't discuss substantive differences with his GOP rivals, so he quickly devised nicknames to define them before we ever had to think about what they were saying. The nicknames stuck, and he rendered meaningful debate irrelevant. Trump's aggressive certainty not only protected him from having to argue facts that were beyond his knowledge, it also preserved his delusions of omniscience.

Certainty figures prominently in another major consequence of Trump's language challenges—his reliance on binary thinking. While the prospect of not thinking holds appeal to everyone, it's especially appealing to people who primarily use binary thinking because they don't feel guilty about further limiting their need to think.

Binary thinking originates from the baby's normal needs to manage his chaotic inner world by dividing his early experiences into distinct and mutually exclusive categories—warm and cold, for example, or positive and negative—which helps clarify experiences that might otherwise be confusing, and defends against fears of chaos or emotional ambiguity. When this primitive reliance on "either/or" distinctions persists into adulthood, however, more complicated thoughts and feelings may be excluded, beyond the grasp of the binary thinker. And those who rely exclusively on binary thinking cannot understand people who think in more nuanced and complex ways.

As binary thinking continues to compromise one's ability

to process complex thoughts, it leads to an unconscious attack on reality—avoiding or destroying the painful self-recognition of whatever hateful feelings or sadistic behaviors one is enacting. This kind of thinking makes flexibility impossible and distorts complexity into a source of danger to be avoided or evaded. One can only use projection to get rid of bad feelings but never can take responsibility for having them.

Trump still is dominated by binary thinking, needing to polarize groups into red and blue, good and bad, legal and illegal—and, perhaps more than any other distinction, winners and losers. What often ensue are quick decisions, because Trump's reality is only defined this way. Options cloud the picture, throwing a wrench into his binary thought process. People who see multiple sides to a particular problem make binary thinkers anxious, forcing a retreat into their either/or world. Evading the pain of complexity stifles emotional and intellectual growth. To hear Trump's binary thinking in action is to hear the sound of arrested emotional and intellectual development—such as when he serially inserted "wrong" to claims he wanted to deny during his second debate with Hillary Clinton, or when in the next debate he countered her charges of collusion with Putin with the memorable "not a puppet, not a puppet, you're a puppet."

This style of thinking has predictably dangerous consequences. The ability to think diplomatically, for example, is compromised when the basic building blocks of diplomacy—listening, talking, and thinking—are beyond one's capacity or are experienced as sources of anxiety rather than as tools for forging connection and finding relief.

Long-term, the individual with language disabilities will be able only to react in situations where explanations are required or demanded. He will rely more heavily on acting without thinking, rather than face the uncertainty of considering different possibilities. We saw in the White House personnel changes of spring 2018 that Trump was able to tolerate fewer and fewer people around him who might press him to think. At the same time, he irritably relies even more on *Fox & Friends* for information and thought. The attraction to non-thought is rooted in the simple, common fact that it's easier to cling to the familiar than to struggle with new ideas. The individual indulging in non-thought may think that he has thought things through, but instead is simply reacting while avoiding the work of thinking. He jumps to conclusions, since feeling certain gives relief. Trump is able to reverse positions so quickly because he never truly holds positions; instead, impaired by his chronic and untreated linguistic challenges, he seizes positions for the purpose of finding the relief that comes with the feeling of certainty, then seizes another perhaps contradictory position when the relief proves to be temporary.

The list of positions that Trump has reversed himself on during his short presidency underscores the challenge of attempting to negotiate with him. His claims of negotiating prowess notwithstanding, Trump functions in a binary perspective that inhibits thought and compromise, which are requisites for successful negotiation. Living in a win-or-lose world, he cannot imagine compromise. Compromise makes him anxious, and anxiety is bad and must be evacuated. Thus he must pull out of climate and trade agreements that were in place when he took office, because remaining in them would require living with a level of complexity that he cannot tolerate.

Yet another consequence of Trump's language disorder is an inability to link cause and effect, except in idiosyncratic ways. Trump can completely ignore something he said the day before—or even minutes before—because whatever he says at the moment is true and correct as far as he is concerned. Trump lives completely in the present: he is a digital thinker, not analog—functioning like a digital watch rather than one with a twelve-hour face and a sweeping second hand that links events in the arc of time. Children do not develop a sense of time until they mourn—experiencing loss is necessary for us to appreciate past and future. Trump says that's not how he works, that he always lives in the present.

For Trump, events and thoughts are segmented, and each experience is unique. Still, he latches on to one or two events that link some of his thoughts—just to make personal sense. It comes out as gibberish to the listener but feels clear to the speaker. Trump really felt he was making sense when he spoke with a bilateral group of lawmakers about DACA: "I think what we are all saying is we'll do DACA and we can

certainly start comprehensive immigration reform the following afternoon, okay?" Trump said. "We'll take an hour off and
start. I do believe that. Because once we get DACA done if it's
done properly with security and everything else, if it's done
properly, we have taken a big chunk of comprehensive out of
the negotiations. I don't think it's going to be that complicated." Trump's Easter 2018 tirade that DACA was dead reflects how stress compromises both his thinking and his
ability to contain frustration; not coincidentally, as he spewed
irrational venom about Mexicans coming across the border to
get DACA, he was standing next to his wife, Melania, whose
reaction to the Stormy Daniels revelations had been widely reported to be a significant source of additional stress on Trump.

The inability to make links is called paramnesia—a distur-
bance of memory that confuses facts and fantasy. For example,
there's scant evidence that he ever understood what DACA is
about, other than that President Obama had instituted it. In
adults we associate this problem with alcoholism or early de-
mentia, as often it's accompanied by memory gaps filled by
made-up stories. Fantasies and paranoid fears dominate
Trump's memory. The news media becomes an easy target for
him, since their memory invariably differs from his and whatever they say is "fake." But Trump remains the person confusing facts with fantasies. Low frustration tolerance is a natural
accompaniment to paramnesia; word finding and remembering become challenging. Lashing out becomes easier.

Being president puts added stress on Trump's thinking;

previously he was never scrutinized like this, as he's called to account for every word or inconsistency. Despite all this, Trump claims he never lies or forgets, though occasionally acknowledges using "truthful hyperbole." In a mid-March 2018 private meeting with donors, he finally admitted that he lied to a foreign leader, Canadian Prime Minister Justin Trudeau. He even bragged about it. Later he said his lie was true after all, and that America does have a trade-deficit problem with Canada. His explanation of why he was correct was itself wrong, leaving him still living in a fantasy fact-free world.

Trump, like all paramnesics, cannot tolerate being corrected. When paramnesic people seem to understand what they are told, they then deny that they ever said anything contrary. At a deep level they attack inner truth by passively resisting it. In Donald Trump's confabulation, we see typical selective behavior—whatever conveys hated truth is usually denied. Trump compulsively lies about his personal life, as well as his presidential responsibilities. He clearly doesn't understand how government works, despite being told frequently. His critics attack him for lying or for being weak, but it's not that simple, because he cannot make links or understand everything that's being said to him. It all sounds good at the time.

Ultimately, Trump's confinement to a simplified, binary world has an unexpected effect on the rest of us: he turns us into a nation of parents. Like a big child relentlessly shouting his frustrations for all to hear, threatening to harm the entire household, Trump places the nation in the position of having to contain him. The United States of America is ill-equipped to cope with a dyslexic president who leads by impulse and who seeks to divide. Donald's biological parents were not equipped either, but his father at least had the option of removing him from the household and isolating him at military school, which provided the structure and order young Donald needed to learn to function with the challenges that his language-processing disorder presented. Unfortunately, the nation lacks a comparable option. The problems we're seeing in the adult Donald Trump are often picked up in the first or second grade, but the impression that young Donny made in his mid-century Queens classroom landed him in the principal's office rather than in an educational consultant's office. His behavior was so disruptive that he required more limit setting than understanding. The same might be true of him today.

THE END OF
THE BEGINNING

He who knows syphilis knows medicine.

⁓ *Sir William Osler*

S
ir William Osler is a hero to a great many in the medical field. Regarded as the father of modern medicine,
Osler practiced in the late nineteenth and early twentieth cen-
turies, before penicillin reduced many a deadly pestilence to a
treatable, curable illness. Before antibiotics, one of the most
unwanted afflictions was syphilis—feared by the patient because it was incurable, and dreaded by the physician because
it was so hard to diagnose. So wide was the range of other ail-
ments that syphilis could cause or imitate—including arthri-
tis, pneumonia, madness, and more—that Osler famously made
the point that the physician who studies all of its possible side
effects and misdiagnoses will ultimately learn about virtually
every disease known to medicine at the time.

I've often thought of Osler as this study of President
Trump's mental state has deepened and expanded to include

so many psychic afflictions. As we've seen, Trump's unconscious has proved to be endlessly resourceful in its development of defenses and coping mechanisms to compensate for what in retrospect was a perfect psychic storm of childhood wounds, conditions, and circumstances. Our attempt to understand his sometimes-confounding state of mind has at times resembled a psychiatry textbook in its seemingly unending array of conditions and disorders. To paraphrase Dr. Osler, he who knows Trump knows psychiatry.

A working knowledge of psychiatric disorders is essential to understanding Trump. The language of psychoanalysis has become a remarkably central element in the national conversation about Trump that continues to dominate the media. While much of the biographical focus on Donald Trump's early life has centered on his relationship to his tyrannical father, I am convinced that Donald experienced unusual and determinative challenges and losses in relationship to his mother, even before he was old enough to walk and talk. The man we now see before us is an adult with an infantilized worldview: a frightened child who is hungry—for power, for fast food, for admiration, for money, for loyalty. He surveys the world around him with uncanny radar for any aspersion, seeing everything but understanding nothing. I think Trump never got over his hurt and rage at not having had a deep preverbal bond with his mother, and the confidence-building joys that warmth, tenderness, touch, scent, or smiles might bring.

He has been angry and determined to get his due ever since, spending his life trying to reach his idealized mother.

When concluding my previous presidential studies, I have posed the hypothetical question of what I would do if I treated the book's subject as my patient. I imagined numerous questions I might ask Trump, but in the spring of 2018, events put a different, new spin on all those hypothetical questions. First, Trump's White House physician Ronny Jackson suffered a devastating public humiliation after a surprise and unlikely nomination to become secretary of veterans affairs. Shortly thereafter, Trump's previous private doctor Harold Bornstein revealed details of a harrowing and perhaps illegal records-seizing raid on his office—along with a confession that the letter in which he purportedly gave Trump a clean bill of health two years prior had in fact been dictated by Trump himself. Suddenly it was clear that treating Donald Trump was a risky proposition.

Jackson's nomination for a job for which he demonstrated minimal credentials was widely perceived as a result of his enthusiastic, credibility-challenging assessment of Trump's health a few months prior, in which evidence suggested that Jackson had misstated Trump's height and weight to avoid his being labeled obese. The raid on Bornstein's office closely followed his reporting that he had treated Trump with Propecia, a popular medicine prescribed to prevent male-pattern baldness. Jackson was ostensibly being rewarded, but he was cast into a Senate confirmation process that appeared from the outset to be doomed to failure (and which Trump immediately said that he wouldn't subject himself to if he were Jackson). Bornstein compared the raid on his office, conducted by a team including Trump's longtime bodyguard and one of his attorneys, to a rape, and risked professional ruin by revealing the origin of the letter he made public. Both doctors had tried to help Trump and ended up worse off; both colluded with Trump in misrepresenting the way he measured and presented his health and appearance, and learned the hard way that individuals who collude with Trump end up paying a price.

Does Trump treat his medical team through a system of punishment and reward tied to something as superficial as his own illusions about his appearance? The highly developed narcissistic impulses that we have observed in Trump would indicate that such a thing is certainly possible. But we've also seen enough about how Trump operates unconsciously to realize that his doctors found themselves at risk of repercussion because of something bigger: they knew the truth about the lies Trump tells himself about himself. To entrust a doctor with one's medical (or psychiatric) treatment is to give the doctor access to intimate, private truths. Trump is so invested in keeping those truths from himself, let alone from others, that it should come as no surprise that the individuals who gain that knowledge are ultimately experienced as a threat to his illusion—and delusion—and end up suffering as a result of it.

This is of interest to me not simply because, for discussion's sake, I might imagine a scenario in which I am the doctor and Trump is the patient; this is of interest because Trump has created a dynamic in which we all serve as his therapists. Similar to how Trump has put the nation in the position of having to parent an under-evolved child of a president, he has turned us into a nation of analysts, constantly on the lookout for signs of further psychic disintegration. If the fates of Trump's own doctors—and lawyers, and advisers, and spokespeople, and even supporters—are any indication, it is a position that comes with considerable risks. The ideas in *Trump on the Couch* are intended to equip the reader with the analytic tools that can help make sense of Trump moving forward. And it's a responsibility that requires each of us to face his own "inner" Trumps—the parts of each of us we'd rather not think about. It's a responsibility we as Americans can't afford to evade, even if it leads us to truths and insights that Trump finds threatening.

By now the reader may have already crafted the insights in these pages into a set of lenses through which to view the president's behavior in an instructive, psychoanalytic light. His April 2018 phone call to *Fox & Friends*, for example, offered vivid illustrations of several concepts the reader might recognize. In his first television appearance in several months, calling into the show the same morning that Admiral Jackson withdrew from consideration for the VA post, Trump struck many viewers as simply and frighteningly unhinged. But revisiting that disturbing appearance from the perspectives developed in these pages, we recognize patterns with which we are now familiar, including: an impulse to blame others for any problems he encounters (in this case the Democrats); a concerning escalation of cognitive limitations (his inability to follow the thread of a conversation); a reminder that in Trump's perspective the "other" is always viewed as bad, dirty, or destructive (in this case James Comey, CNN, and Robert Mueller); and the continued paranoid portrayal of himself as victim. Also on prominent display was the now-familiar disconnect between Trump's language, meaning, and the truth, most conspicuously when he contradicted himself mid-rant while railing against his perceived enemies on "fake news" networks: "I don't watch them at all. I watched last night."

Perhaps most troubling was the relentlessness with which Trump's tone grew ever angrier, threatening at times to escape his control and explode into full-throated rage. Phoning into the relative calm of morning talk television, Trump sounded out of place in the elevated dudgeon that plays so well at his rallies. Presumably calling from the privacy of his White House retreat, the off-camera Trump attacked his familiar targets with mounting agitation, as his remote audience of the three *Fox & Friends* hosts tried to maintain calm on-screen. The same destructive impulses to which he gives such free expression from the rally podium sounded more out of control when coming from an isolated, disembodied voice— as if Trump's familiar destructive impulses somehow posed a greater risk to Trump himself without the presence of a live, adoring audience to reflect and join him in his rage.

The looks on the hosts' faces suggested they knew they were failing to contain Trump's rage. Their discomfort also betrayed their growing realization of just how badly the president needed to be contained. The less they were able to contain him, the more agitated Trump became. They kept trying to change the topic in an apparent attempt to distract the president from erupting into full-blown chaos. Without their knowing it, they were unconsciously attempting to serve as the human equivalent of the wall, the psychic skin that Trump's disordered personality relies upon to keep him from falling apart entirely. But Trump needs the collusion of a co-pacetic crowd to keep his rage from overtaking him. The *Fox & Friends* hosts' calm had the opposite effect. Instead of acting as a wall, their efforts simply highlighted how desperately Trump needs to be walled in. After their attempts to contain him continued to fail, they ended the conversation before he got even worse on their watch.

The confrontation would have proved challenging for any trained mental health professional. Presumably following control-room instructions, the hosts eventually cut Trump off, just as he was revving up for another round of invective against Comey, the FBI, and the Clinton Foundation. The timing of the shutdown was not apparent, as it had been clear since early in the interview that Fox News's favorite president was not showing himself to his best advantage that morning and was clearly out of control. (Later on MSNBC, Lawrence O'Donnell speculated that the unilateral decision to end the interview required the intervention of network News Corp Executive Chairman Rupert Murdoch himself.) But moments before he abruptly ended the interview, *Fox & Friends* cohost Brian Kilmeade had exposed a central element to the dynamic that had previously remained hidden. Interrupting Trump's tirade against the "council of seven people" on CNN, of which Trump said, "every one is against me," host Kilmeade offered, "I'm not your doctor, Mr. President, but I would—I would recommend you watch less of them."

With the possible exception of Sean Hannity's Fox News broadcast, there is no television media environment more solicitous and sympathetic to Trump and his presidency than *Fox & Friends*. Multiple studies have tracked the correlation between *Fox & Friends* slants on the news and Trump's tweets, which regularly and at times immediately echo their stories. It's clear from the transcript that Trump was incapable that morning of simultaneously appearing on the show and listening closely to what was being said. But if Kilmeade had said something comparable to another guest while Trump was watching, it's easy to imagine what Trump's take on it would have been: the fact that the host was so exasperated by the mental state of his guest that he introduced the notion of how a doctor might address the guest's volatile mind-set would have been heard by Trump as confirmation of that guest's instability. Instead, the suggestion that Trump could use—and perhaps even has—a doctor to help him maintain mental stability was unacknowledged. Instead, Trump retorted with the earlier-mentioned defensive contradiction—"I don't watch them at all. I watched last night"—at which point cohost Steve Doocy attempted unsuccessfully to stifle a laugh.

The question about Trump's mental health and the possible need for treatment has been a topic for public discussion that predates his presidency, and it will continue long past his presidency. Much of that initial discussion came from the political Left, then expanded into what remains of the center. But if that discussion is now reverberating in the pro-Trump, conservative media echo chamber exemplified by *Fox & Friends*, then it has reached a whole new level. If Fox News is suggesting that the president's moods could benefit from medical attention, there's no telling who is next.

As this manuscript was being delivered to its publisher, Trump was sounding more unstable than ever. At no point has there been any evidence that Trump's mental health is going to improve. Rather, indications suggest that his psychic state is deteriorating and will likely continue to get worse and more widely discussed. Any survey of his mental health conducted at this point will thus inevitably feel incomplete; in that respect, the book I never expected to write has become the book I never expect to finish.

The work of assessing the president's mental health will go on. The goal of this study has never been to diagnose but to observe, comprehend, and provide some context, to improve our understanding of the characteristics of Trump's behavior. In other words, *Trump on the Couch* has endeavored to offer the beginning of an education in psychiatric principles that will help add depth and structure to concerns about the state of the president's mental health. An educated reader, one hopes, is a reader who is empowered, motivated, and even inspired.

Simply becoming an educated reader can be seen as an act of defiance against a president who audaciously proclaimed on the campaign trail, "I love the poorly educated." Education can put one at odds with Trump's supporters as well: the poorly educated voters returned Trump's love, awarding him victories in forty-three of the nation's fifty least-educated counties in 2016 (and only ten of the fifty most-educated). Trump's pathology flourishes when unchallenged by awareness or insight. Information is power, but it is also a responsibility.

Nothing about studying Trump's psyche has reduced my concern about his fitness for office. The more I learned, and the deeper I looked, my conviction that he is a menace to himself and his people grew ever stronger. This knowledge has only raised my anxiety, an effect I suspect it will have on many readers too. But anxiety, though unpleasant, is not something we have to run away from. Anxiety is a source of information, and in that respect is a responsibility as well.

This book is not a personal attack on Trump, nor is it a rebuttal to some of his messages, because that would overlook the genuine grievances Trump supporters have with Washington elites in general and the Obama administration in

particular. These are real and passionate feelings of disloca-
tion and impotence, to which Trump has given voice. This
book is a call to action for all Americans, because Trump reminds us of what happens when anxiety is denied or ignored.
He is consumed and misled by a lifetime of unprocessed, unacknowledged anxiety, which has no doubt been exacerbated
by the power and responsibility of his office. Trump challenges us to avoid making the same mistakes. The work begun
in these pages must continue.

GLOSSARY

Neurosis is the inability to tolerate ambiguity.

— *Sigmund Freud*

B elow are some of the psychoanalytic terms and ideas that informed my approach to President Trump.

Containment is what a mother or other primary caretaker does to harbor and think about her baby's feelings—especially when the baby is angry or frightened. The mother experiences what the baby projects onto her and transforms it into a response, such as feeding or changing or cuddling the baby. It is a process of taking feelings in during maternal reverie, and transforming them into action. This process over time is internalized by the baby, who develops his own capacity to take feelings from others—to understand them and respond to them. Maternal containment emerges from the harmonious mix-up between mother and child, often called the nursing couple or mother-child union. Donald Trump at his rallies often spreads his arms in a maternal way, as if he's containing the crowd's feelings, their projected needs and frustrations, before transforming them into promises to act—like build a wall, drain the swamp, or ban Muslim immigrants. The process of containing helps the baby develop confidence in his environment, much the way Trump's supporters develop confidence in him as their leader and protector who understands them.

The containing process evolves over time so the baby can experience the containing function in the rest of the family and eventually from society at large. An anxious caregiver has trouble being in proper attunement with her baby—and a hyperactive baby may feel that the mother isn't there to soothe him, even when she is trying very hard. The issue, then, is not simply that the mother is an inadequate container, but also that the baby may be unable to be contained, something we see in babies who have severe colic or are extremely fidgety. Donald Trump was a very fidgety baby.

A containing leader is able to think about what comes his or her way and not immediately react to it—especially when a particular issue is dominated by extreme anxiety. Candidate Trump reassured his supporters that he would "make America great again," like a containing parent might respond to needs and fears. He also promised to protect supporters from outsiders who he said wanted to take away our belongings, jobs, and freedoms.

Displacement is a basic law of unconscious functioning, namely unconscious shifting or transferring unpleasant memories or images from their primary source onto something or someone in the here and now. For example, President Trump may be displacing onto his political critics like Chuck Schumer or Nancy Pelosi the distrust he felt toward his teachers who sent him to the principal's office for his disruptive classroom behavior. The unconscious law of displacement is that it helps keep the original sources of anger hidden from conscious memory, thereby allowing feelings to be reactive to current situations. This mental process also facilitates racism and sexism because one needs some group to blame for one's frustrations.

Dissociation means the separation of one part of the mind—or self—from another. For example, Trump has demonstrated that he is both a builder and a destroyer: he wants to build greatness in America, while destroying the essential government institutions like the FBI or EPA that make it great. Dissociation comes into play when Trump sees himself as only the builder, thinking that what he's destroying is in the service of what he's building. Emotional health results from bringing dissociated parts of the self together.

Trump's dissociation disconnects his memory of cause and effect, of fact and fantasy. It allows him to say one thing and do another. His about-face on gun control after the Parkland shooting is a good example of dissociation.

Dissociation is linked to the concept of *false self*. Childhood emotional injury can often lead to the creation of a persistent false self. Young Donald presented a false self as a bully and a know-it-all. Because Donald Trump was a television celebrity before he entered politics, he already had access to a ready-made false self he could assume as a candidate and president. For Trump, tapping into this false self is like getting dressed up a certain way for a party, except the party never ends.

Dyslexia is a learning disorder that can have a profound impact on the personality, on one's ability both to organize and to control one's impulses. This disorder is usually recognized when the child has trouble learning to read and spell in elementary school. Dyslexia is a language-processing disorder that compromises the abilities to understand meaning, experience empathy, and regulate self-esteem. The dyslexic child may develop grandiose fantasies that exaggerate and distort his abilities. These children can't sit still; their minds wander when they don't understand, and then they stop listening entirely. This is often how ADHD (attention deficit hyperactive disorder) is first detected. But sometimes the diagnosis of dyslexia isn't made until adulthood, and one clue is frequently misspelled words—something we see regularly in Trump's Twitter production.

While the source of trouble is neurological, the child's problems become psychological. Donald Trump's simplistic language reflects his difficulty thinking about his feelings, which leads him instead just to react. Dyslexic children often exhibit delayed social skills, which might account for Trump's discomfort in groups where he's just a member and not the leader. This may contribute to his hatred of international treaties, because they involve give-and-take. He needs "executive time" alone. People with dyslexia also get easily overstimulated cognitively and emotionally.

Envy is the angry feeling that someone else has something desirable that you don't have, accompanied by an impulse to take it away or spoil it. For instance, President Trump envies that Hillary Clinton won the popular vote or that Obama's inauguration crowd was so large. His rageful disputing of those facts protects him from psychic pain. *Envy* is often used interchangeably with *jealousy*, but they are not the same. Where jealousy is about three people, envy is about only two. Jealousy has to do initially with Oedipal feelings in which the child wants to possess one parent and exclude the other. Babies get jealous when their mother is on the phone with someone, and might try to take the phone away from her. Envy is an expression of hate, not love mixed with hate. It is about hating something another person has. Both emotions can lead to violence and destruction, however. Years ago I had a patient who described her feelings clearly to me. I told her I was going on holiday and she responded that she felt both envious and jealous. She envied that it seemed easier for me to leave her than for her to leave me, and she was jealous that I was going away with someone else and not with her.

Jealousy is based on love; envy is not. People manage envy in ways other than pure destructiveness. By bragging, they try to get others to envy them—so they can project their own envious feelings onto someone else. Trump parades beautiful women to be envied; Michael Wolff wrote that Trump liked seducing wives of his friends to spoil their marriages but that he wasn't overtly jealous—he envied his friends their wives and their happy marriages.

Grandiosity is a fantasy that compensates for a lost sense of perfection, protecting against disappointment. If a child feels shamed or dismissed, he may internally construct a grandiose self to love. But that self is never enough, and requires the regular replenishment we see President Trump constantly pursuing. He provides his own replenishment as well, reminding us that he has the "best words," for example, or declaring in a reference to foreign policy issues, "The only one that matters is me. I'm the only one that matters," as he said in November 2017.

Hyperbole—Trump introduced his idea of "truthful hyperbole" in *The Art of the Deal*. Of course, hyperbole is by definition not the truth, so he is asserting the impossible existence of truthful lies. In the unconscious, hyperbole reflects rivalry, envy, and disavowal—those who use it are fundamentally competitive and also defending against feeling envy. Fowler's *Modern English Usage* is closer to what Trump says hyperbole is—an exaggeration "not meant to be taken literally." When Trump modifies *hyperbole* with the word *truthful,* he is describing what he still does as president—he says things that he says are true, while at the same time tells us not to take him literally. The essence of his chaos is contained in that self-disclosed phrase—one he is proud of.

Idealization is the product of extreme splitting, beyond the simple internal world of good and bad, and into one that is ideal and awful. It transforms the perception of reality into something better; it may lay dormant in the unconscious and emerge when one falls in love or has a baby. Just as lovers see themselves—their best selves—in another, the electorate usually idealizes their candidate for higher office. Thus Ann Coulter sounded like a betrayed lover when Trump signed a budget that didn't include funding for the wall he promised her. When people feel understood by a leader—or by a therapist—they idealize that person. Trump's base felt that he understood their frustration and pent-up rage, so they idealized him more than any American president in decades. He promised to "drain the swamp" and destroy the self-centered elites. They idealized him so much that he said he could shoot someone on Fifth Avenue and not lose a vote, and no one corrected or contradicted him. They loved him: never have there been such long lines at campaign rallies as there were at Trump's. He tapped into unconscious recall of the infant's love for the parent, who can magically understand the child even before he has words.

Identification with the aggressor, at its simplest, is when an abused child abuses someone weaker. Their dynamic is often the source of bullying, as the bully had a bullying parent (or two) and projects the contemptible disavowed weak self onto weaker people he can then treat badly.

Object is a neutral term for a person whom one loves or hates, or may eventually love *and* hate. Objects are internal constructs we make of the people with whom we relate. Thus we have good objects, bad objects, and whole objects about which we have "mixed feelings." Internally we relate to these objects in a variety of ways, and those relationships can help or hinder how we experience getting along with the real (or "material") people in our lives. Thus we have our internal reality that interacts with material reality—and internal objects that interact with material ones. An *autocratic* object is created by a child with a tyrannical parent—and often blocks his ability to learn and grow because it feels dangerous to the child to do so, to surpass his parent. An autocratic object may compromise learning, which can result in symptoms that teachers label as dyslexia. In those cases, intensive therapy with the child may help him gain enough perspective on and distance from his internal autocratic object that he can be free to learn again. Trump never had therapy that might have addressed his childhood difficulties, and instead remains bound to his internal tormenter, coping with it by displacement and projection onto Robert Mueller, or by his paranoid reactions to the media.

Persecution—A vivid example of persecution is when a two-year-old child is awakened by night terrors, fearful that there is some form of menace in the room—monsters, ghosts, heavy storms, or attacking dogs. All these are forms of projected aggression. In order to rid himself of his inner aggression, the child tries to outsource it, becoming afraid of the dark, for example, or of being attacked. When the mother disappoints, the baby projects his aggression and rage onto her and then fears her, a process similar to paranoia. The baby feels persecuted. Adults can have childhood feelings of persecution activated—as we see with excessive fears of immigrants taking away jobs.

Preconception—A belief, idea, or theory formed before it's tested is considered a preconception. While preconceptions can be altered or confirmed, depending on what is experienced, some people, such as President Trump, prefer to avoid experiences that challenge their long-held beliefs—so they are reluctant to try new ideas or accept social change as something that might be good. Trump has a preconception that interdependence in international trade is like being taken advantage of—and nothing can convince him differently.

It feels risky to have preconceptions challenged; for example, in the idea that government takes away our freedoms by overregulating them, those feelings are experienced as facts but could be seen as preconceptions if a new realization occurs, such as the fact that government regulation protects clean water against polluters. But if we see all preconceptions as facts, then we turn away from searching for truth. That search is as necessary for the psyche as food is for the body—without it, the psyche starves. Trump is dominated by preconceptions, and when anyone on his staff challenges one, it seems he would rather fire them than listen.

Projection—As used most commonly in this study, projection is the attribution of tendencies, desires, or motives to someone else in order not to recognize that they come from inside. In this dynamic, the individual typically projects his unlikable or dishonorable qualities. If acknowledged in oneself, these qualities would cause anxiety; when projected outside, they can cause the individual to feel anxious about what someone else might do.

Regression is a return to a previous life situation to escape anxiety caused by the present. When reverting to earlier forms of thought, such as the way a child might have perceived his world, the individual is conscious of his emotions while unconscious of their original source. Trump's constant rage at the Mueller investigation suggests that he has returned to his anger at his father for sending him away to military school for his secret forbidden trips into Manhattan. The situation with Mueller is far more complex, but President Trump's feelings are regressed and simplified into the way he felt toward his father. He is regressed without awareness of the source of his fury; he just wants to fire Mueller, an impulse close to an unremembered Oedipal urge he must have once had to kill his father. Unfortunately for Trump, the simplified level of psychic functioning that accompanies a regressed state makes it harder for him to consider the consequences of his actions.

Repetition compulsion is an unconscious drive to put oneself into stressful situations. It often invites regression as well. Each time Trump unconsciously invited Mueller to investigate, for example, he repeated his historic struggle with his father, although Trump experiences it as being only about current circumstances.

President Trump promised DACA reform to Democrats before taking it back. When he rescinds promises, he's repeating something he learned very early in life when he got his little brother, Robert, to lend him his building blocks—Donny never returned them and instead glued them together to make a taller tower. He won that one but continued to flirt with disaster until he was finally sent away to New York Military Academy.

The need to continue to make the world around him chaotic while putting himself in yet another precarious position is repetition compulsion—and it functions with Trump in paradoxical ways. He puts his base into the position of Robert, inviting their trust, and he puts his opposition into states of anxiety and fear—also something he did to Robert. The compulsive part is that Trump is doing something out of his conscious control, a pattern of cruel seduction followed by keeping what was consciously given—love and trust that he'd build a wall—for himself and from his base. He repeats his fears of his father coupled with his need to make his father anxious (remember that Fred Trump was on the board of Donny's elementary school and often heard about his son's violent disruptive behavior). Everything looks like a present-day conflict and nothing like a reenactment of his core childhood struggle. And it's both.

Sadism—Sadism is basically sexualized aggression, getting erotic pleasure at inflicting pain on others. Excessive sadism can inhibit learning and curiosity, because the desire to inflict pain is much more easily realized if the person doing it knows very little about the humanity of his or her object (victim). The sadist will unconsciously choose to learn less and less over time in order to sustain an angry destructive worldview. Trump maintains that view, and it has driven his decisions to streamline his cabinet much like he did his private business—people were there not just to praise him but also not to challenge his decisions. Trump expresses his sadism with an element of cowardice, firing cabinet members with a tweet from afar, after sweet-talking them into thinking their relationship was fine. His behavior toward our allies is sadistic, as he seems to enjoy making them distraught about the likelihood he'll scuttle the Iran nuclear treaty. He prefers doing what he wants over doing what he must—and what he often wants to do is to inflict cruelty on others.

Splitting describes the primitive psychological process of dividing our external and internal worlds into good and bad.

When the baby has good feelings of being held and loved, everything is good; when he has colic or rage, everything is bad. We split our experiences into good and bad to protect one feeling from the other. Infants and young children cannot believe that the same object that caused a great experience can cause a hated experience. As good experiences with good objects build up, the bad experiences become more tolerable, and eventually the baby feels strong enough internally so that good feelings outweigh bad ones. Over time we identify with our internal good objects and they become part of ourselves. For Trump, this process was about making himself *the* loved object, the most trustworthy one of all. Rather than either of his parents, he was the good object he loved. The split-off "bad" Trump had trouble learning, resulting in too much envious hatred to take in positive experiences. Over time, this split weakened his capacity to love or to feel good about the world in which he lived.

Transference and ***countertransference*** are the terms fundamental to our thinking about the issues raised in *Trump on the Couch*. Therefore, discussing this particular set of definitions may seem more like a chapter than a specific term—sort of the way one week of President Trump seems more like a year.

Transference is the basic tool used by the analyst in psychoanalytic treatment, and consists of displacements of impulses and feelings from the past onto the present. In treatment, these feelings are directed toward the analyst. In life outside the consulting room, they are directed toward one's spouse, children, boss, or colleagues. Adults understandably live in the present and rarely think that things driving their feelings might also stem from forgotten past experiences.

Using the lens of applied psychoanalysis, I can speculate about possible sources of what President Trump feels about people in his current life—especially his wife and children, his White House staff, reporters in the media, and particular figures like Kelly, Sessions, and Mueller. I look at what might be President Trump's internal fantasies that influence those relationships. He also has relationships to institutions such as the FBI, CIA, Supreme Court, Congress, and the NRA—all of which are colored by his unconscious fantasies.

Transference feelings influence how we experience every new relationship, including readers' feelings toward Trump before reading this book; what readers feel after finishing the book may be less dominated by preconceptions and hopefully be enriched. What we transfer onto Trump are myriad feelings and defenses that influence our perceptions. I've had difficulties modifying my own preconceptions about him during this process.

Because Trump was a celebrity known to many Americans before he ran for president, our perception of him is partly based on his appearances on *The Apprentice*. To New Yorkers, transference to Trump was more intense because they knew him as a builder whose buildings dwarfed old skyscrapers and who was in regular contact with the press, often interviewed by Howard Stern, and also the subject of numerous lawsuits. To many Americans before he ran for president, our perception of him was originally based in large part on transference of our own hopes, fears, and expectations. If the trauma of 9/11, augmented by recent terrorist attacks worldwide, aroused fears of Muslims in general, we might be drawn to a candidate who proposed banning all Muslim immigrants until our immigration screening was made better. We might interpret his demands to build a wall as protecting us—or others of us might feel that Trump wants to cut us off from the rest of the world. Some of those feelings depend on our own internal world and how that provides each of us a unique view of Candidate Trump as well as President Trump. The seeds of who he is had already been planted in our minds before he started running, and complicated our abilities to form genuine first impressions.

If we need to have a president who functions as a reassuring parental figure, we might feel threatened by his vengefulness as well as his huge shifts in policy decisions. If we want to feel safe knowing that a mature person has his hands on the nuclear button, we might be more anxious than in recent memory. If some of us had been abused as children, or had our boundaries disrespected or ignored, we might be paranoid about President Trump. If we had parents who spent all their time entertaining or being away from home for work or other reasons, we might feel connected to Trump because he regularly attacks Washington elites who stand for those indifferent parents.

Transference feelings intensify during times of stress—individual or cultural—when people often resort to old solutions to new problems, applying the familiar to help modify their anxiety of confronting the unknown, as well as to solve problems in ways more tried-and-true, even if the resolution wasn't always the best one.

We may also transfer denied or unremembered parts of ourselves as children onto another person and then react to that person as if he weren't listening or didn't really understand our frustration. I had a patient who, no matter what I said, felt I didn't get him. I got frustrated as well and started to feel that he wouldn't let me help him. I suddenly thought of my mother, who insisted on doing everything herself, not letting me participate in daily household life. Suddenly I saw that I was having similar feelings about Hillary Clinton, who kept insisting on her slogan, "I'm with her," when I wanted my patient to be with me working together. I wished Clinton would have said, "We're with each other." This leads to discussing *countertransference*, or of my feelings toward the patient and thus toward a candidate (Hillary) who didn't seem to listen.

Countertransference, the transference feelings the therapist has toward his or her patient, comprises expectations from the therapist's own past experiences as well as feelings that are specific to a patient's particular transference. I found myself doing extra tidying in my consulting room before the arrival of a particular patient—something that obviously had to do with my countertransference feelings that his transferences provoked in me. It was as if I expected him to yell at me for being messy. What I transferred from my past was an experience of having been disorganized as a child and being scolded because of it. This patient's expectation that I always be punctual and neat was from a feeling he had when he was a child, since his own mother was invariably late picking him up from basketball practice. But I felt self-conscious and almost tyrannically scrutinized by him lest I make a mistake. He could never have made such demands on his mother, but the enraged dominant part of him came out in our work together. So there is a powerful interaction between transference and countertransference.

The president has transferences directed at us also. His transference toward the liberals is that they are weak, don't put America first, and let in too many immigrants. He has intense positive transference to the military; the New York Military Academy structured his impulsivity. As president, he appointed military people—some on active duty—to civilian positions in his cabinet. He also hated the media and felt unfairly treated by repressed parental "fake news."

Unconscious—The unconscious is a part of the mind inaccessible to consciousness, and in fact comprises most of mental life. We get access to it indirectly, through dreams and behaviors, and through recovered forgotten memories that are indistinguishable from fantasies, feelings, or wishes.

The unconscious is one's ally more often than most people think; intuition, for example, is one form of unconscious knowledge. After all, survival and growth are fundamental drives that our unconscious helps us realize in ways we can't always consciously recognize. When a good marriage is called a "match made in heaven," for example, it is a match based in part on unconscious knowledge of the other.

The unconscious can also be a cauldron of hurt. Donald Trump faced his own hurts from paternal tyranny and maternal self-absorption to the extent that he could not repair them. Others who get love and attention after having been traumatized may not revisit and inflict their childhood traumas onto their own children, but Trump didn't consciously face or come to terms with his rage at his father—so he imposed a tyranny on his own children similar to his childhood experiences. His children both praise and fear him. Trump's approach to managing his childhood hurts was to externalize them and inflict them on those around him. And now he continues to inflict them on all aspects of American life.

BIBLIOGRAPHY

Alford, C. Fred. *Melanie Klein and Critical Social Theory*. New Haven: Yale University Press, 1989.

Barbu, Zevedei. *Democracy and Dictatorship: Their Psychology and Patterns of Life*. New York: Grove Press, 1959.

Barrett, Wayne. *Trump: The Greatest Show on Earth: The Deals, The Downfall, The Reinvention*. New York: Regan Arts, 1992 & 2016.

Bennett, Michael, and Dave Zirin. *Things That Make White People Uncomfortable*. Chicago: Haymarket Books, 2018.

Bion, W. R. *Attention and Interpretation*. London: Tavistock Publications, 1970.

Blair, Gwenda. *The Trumps: Three Generations of Builders and a President*. New York: Simon & Schuster, 2001.

Bowden, Mark. "Trump and Me: Donald Trump Really Doesn't Want Me to Tell You This, But . . ." *Vanity Fair*. December 2015.

Collins, Nancy. "Donald Trump Talks Family, Women in Unearthed Transcript: 'When I Come Home and Dinner's Not Ready, I Go Through the Roof.'" *The Hollywood Reporter*. October 13, 2016.

Comey, James. *A Higher Loyalty: Truth, Lies, and Leadership*. New York: Flatiron, 2018.

Cruz, Leonard, and Steven Buser, eds. *A Clear and Present Danger: Narcissism in the Era of Donald Trump*. Asheville, North Carolina: Chiron Publications, 2016.

D'Antonio, Michael. *The Truth About Trump.* New York: Thomas Dunne Books/St. Martin's Press, 2015.

Etchegoyen, Horacio. *The Fundamentals of Psychoanalytic Technique.* London: Karnac Books, 1991.

Ferlinghetti, Lawrence. "Mock Confessional" (1973). Bancroft Library, University of California Folder 28, Ferlinghetti Collection.

Fodor, Mandor, and Frank Gaynor, eds. *Freud: Dictionary of Psychoanalysis.* New York: Barnes and Noble, 2004.

Frank, Justin A. "Listening with the Big Ear: A Laingian Approach to Psychotic Families." *Journal of American Academy of Psychoanalysis.* 18(1): 131–144, 1990.

Frank, Justin A. *Bush on the Couch: Inside the Mind of the President.* New York: HarperCollins/ReganBooks, 2004.

Frank, Justin A. *Obama on the Couch: Inside the Mind of the President.* New York: Simon & Schuster/Free Press, 2011.

Freud, Anna. *The Ego and the Mechanisms of Defense.* In: *The Writings of Anna Freud.* Volume 2. London: Hogarth Press, 1965.

Freud, Sigmund. *Civilization and Its Discontents.* London: Hogarth Press, 1930.

Freud, Sigmund. "Some Character Types met in Psychoanalytic Work." In: *The Standard Edition of the Complete Psychological Works of Sigmund Freud.* Translated from the German by James Strachey. Volume 16. London: Hogarth Press, 1970.

Fromm, Erich. *Escape from Freedom.* New York: Holt, 1994.

Green, Joshua. *Devil's Bargain: Steve Bannon, Donald Trump, and the Storming of the Presidency.* New York: Penguin, 2017.

Hartman, Heinz. *Ego Psychology and the Problem of Adaptation.* New York: International Universities Press, 1939.

Hinshelwood, R. D. *A Dictionary of Kleinian Thought.* London: Free Association Books, 1991.

Hofstadter, Richard. *Anti-Intellectualism in American Life.* New York: Vintage, 1963.

The Holy Bible. New York: Oxford University Press, 2002.

Hurt III, Harry. *Lost Tycoon: The Many Lives of Donald J. Trump.* Boston: Norton, 1993.

Johnston, David Cay. *The Making of Donald Trump.* New York: Melville House, 2016.

Johnston, David Cay. *It's Even Worse Than You Think: What the Trump Administration Is Doing to America.* New York: Simon & Schuster, 2018.

Jones, Ernest. "The God Complex (1913)." In: Jones, E., *Essays in Applied Psychoanalysis.* Volume 2. London: Hogarth Press, 1951.

Khazan, Olga. "People Voted for Trump Because They Were Anxious, Not Poor." *The Atlantic.* April 23, 2018.

Klaas, Brian. *The Despot's Apprentice: Donald Trump's Attack on Democracy.* New York: Hot Books, 2017.

Klein, Melanie. *Love, Guilt and Reparation and Other Works 1921–1945.* New York: Macmillan/Free Press, 1975.

Klein, Melanie. *Envy and Gratitude and Other Works 1946–1963.* London: Hogarth Press, 1975.

Kranish, Michael, and Marc Fisher. *Trump Revealed: The Definitive Biography of the 45th President.* New York: Scribner, 2016.

Kruse, Michael. "The Mystery of Mary Trump." *Politico.* November/December 2017.

Kullman, Alitta. *Hunger for Connection: Finding Meaning in Eating Disorders.* New York: Routledge, 2018.

Laplanche, Jean, and Jean-Bertrand, Pontalis. *The Language of Psycho-Analysis.* Translated by Donald Nicholson-Smith. London: Hogarth Press, 1973.

Lawrence, Ken. *The World According to Trump: An Unauthorized Portrait in His Own Words.* Kansas City: Andrews McMeel Publishing, 2005.

Lee, Bandy, ed. *The Dangerous Case of Donald Trump: 27 Psychiatrists and Mental Health Experts Assess the President.* New York: Thomas Dunne Books/St. Martin's Press, 2017.

Levin, Ira. *The Stepford Wives.* New York: Random House, 1972.

Meltzer, Donald, ed. *The Collected Papers of Roger Money-Kyrle*. Aberdeen, Scotland: Roland Harris Educational Trust, 1978.

Melville, Herman. *The Confidence-Man: His Masquerade (1857)*. New York: Penguin Classics, 1991.

O'Brien, Timothy L. *TrumpNation: The Art of Being the Donald*. New York: Grand Central Publishing, 2016.

O'Donnell, John R., with James Rutherford. *Trumped: The Inside Story of the Real Donald Trump—His Cunning Rise and Spectacular Fall*. New York: Simon & Schuster, 1992, and Smashwords, 2016.

Plaskin, Glenn. Interview with Donald Trump. *Playboy*. March 1, 1990.

Segal, Hannah. *Introduction to the Work of Melanie Klein*. New York: Basic Books, 1974.

Singer, Mark. "Trump Solo." *The New Yorker*. May 19, 1997.

Singer, Mark. *Trump and Me*. New York: Tim Duggan Books, 2016.

Spillius, Elizabeth Bott, et al., eds. *The New Dictionary of Kleinian Thought*. London: Routledge, 2011.

Steiner, John. *Psychic Retreats: Pathological Organizations in Psychotic, Neurotic, and Borderline Patients*. London: Routledge, 1993.

Suebsaeng, Asawin. "'You Have to Treat 'Em Like Shit': Before Megyn Kelly, Trump Dumped Wine on a Female Reporter." *Daily Beast*. August 8, 2015.

Symington, Joan (Cornwall). "The Survival Function of Primitive Omnipotence." *International Journal of Psychoanalysis*, 66: 481–7, 1985.

Symington, Neville. *Narcissism: A New Theory*. London: Karnac, 1993.

Trump, Donald J., and Bill Zanker. *Think Big: Make It Happen in Business and Life*. Originally published as *Think Big and Kick Ass in Business and Life*. New York: HarperCollins, 2007.

Trump, Donald J., with Tony Schwartz. *Trump: The Art of the Deal*. New York: Random House, 1987.

Trump, Donald J., with Kate Bohner. *Trump: The Art of the Comeback*. New York: Times Books, 1997.

Trump, Donald J., with Charles Leerhsen. *Trump: Surviving at the Top.* New York: Random House, 1990.

Tuccille, Jerome. *Trump: The Saga of America's Most Powerful Real Estate Baron.* New York: Donald I. Fine, 1985.

Volkan, Vamik. *Blind Trust: Large Groups and Their Leaders in Times of Crisis and Terror.* Charlottesville, Virginia: Pitchstone, 2004.

Wolff, Michael. *Fire and Fury: Inside the Trump White House.* New York: Holt, 2018.

ACKNOWLEDGMENTS

This is my last book analyzing sitting presidents. I cannot think of writing *Pence on the Couch. Trump on the Couch*, as I said in the introduction, is the book I never expected to write. But eventually it became the book I never expect to finish.

I never would have gotten this far without a lot of wonderful support, especially the hands-on help from Tom Spain, Dawn Whitmore, and my wife, Heather. No amount of loving tweets could do any of them justice, or express my deepest gratitude. Tom makes me think, puts things together, challenges me like nobody I've ever met—he also helps the narrative flow and make sense, which is not easy to do with this particular project. Dawn cracks the whip, insisting that I stay on track and push through various hurdles by helping me stay focused. Her loving enthusiasm makes being pushed feel good. And Heather provided just about everything—loving support, tough criticism, keeping the house going, feeding our three dogs, doing research, reading and editing virtually every chapter.

I thank my agent, Gail Ross, who insisted I meet with prospective publishers in New York—and her enthusiasm certainly helped me connect with Avery Books and its smart, challenging, and responsive editor Caroline Sutton. Her regular votes of confidence were more than helpful in this unexpectedly tough slog. And it was an added boost for me to spend time with enthusiastic members of her team, including Anne Kosmoski, Alyssa Kasoff, Alexandra Bruschi, Hannah Steigmeyer, and Janice Kurzius.

It's not easy living in the swamp. Washington, DC, has been home for more than forty years, though it remains ever changing while still being static. Without the enormous help of Bea Tolson, the swamp outside would have overtaken my writing space. I got lots of help while dwelling here: dear friends and colleagues Tito and Nechy Pieczanski provided more insight and intellectual energy than I could ever hope to do on my own. You've always helped me grow, think, and analyze. Nancy Miller is my lively, intelligent, and supportive friend, who pushed me to keep writing when each week felt like two months. Her plush bald eagle still looks over my shoulder when I work. Her dear husband and friend, Walter Romanek, kept the enthusiasm flowing, interspersed with political discussions, dinners, and the occasional opera diversions.

There is a special place in my heart reserved for Steve and Karen Scheinman, Rob and Nina Pobi, and Bob Taraschi, who kept me not only sane but also emotionally solvent. I know I wouldn't have made it without your generosity of spirit and help. A shout-out to Rob for reminding me how hard it is to write, despite my sense that he does it effortlessly. Bob offered me ideas, including a section—not realized, unfortunately—of practical self-help ideas so readers might better cope with President Trump. Steve and Karen took me into their swamp-less haven so I could write for a blissful week.

Humor helps, as do kindred spirits: Harvey Saferstein kept asking me if the book was finished yet; Lou Borgenicht and Jody Plant shared their numerous thoughts about Trump's impact in faraway Utah; Marty Gold and Jacki Meyer welcomed, fed, and housed me on many of my weekend New York trips, where I taught seminars and met with editors. Marty's creative cooking mixed well with his sardonic wit. Luckily I found a second second home in New York as well—that of Charlie Warner and Julia Bradford. They warmly offered mouthwatering breakfasts, as well as astute observations on Trump as a TV personality. Jerry Zupnick, med-school roommate from decades ago, also kept me laughing, though warning me that Pence could be worse (now echoed by, of all people, George Will). Hank Lowenstein emailed absurdly funny pictures that invigorated me on a daily basis.

Other friends and colleagues helped keep the project going, and some of them read chapters: Alitta Kullman, Mark Dawes, and Hannah and Jeff Fox eagerly and critically read bits and pieces. Bill Frischling of Factba.se gave me spreadsheets of Trump's word usage, along with astute linguistic analyses.

I also thank close friends Dr. Ray and Shauna Wertheim, Dr. Judith Nowak, Dr. Carol Ann Dyer, Dr. Paul Steinberg, Dr. Marty and Mary Stein, Carlos Campbell, Sabrina Cassagnol and Chuck Gilligan, Dr. Larry Hill, Bob Kaplan and Marilyn Black, Jesse Kornbluth, Joe Scott and Susan Morgan, Gary Addie, Jenni and Jacob Romanek, Michael Carmichael, Jeremy Mohler, Dr. Mike and Elizabeth Marcus, John and Kaye Spilker, Dr. Irene Roth and Dr. Vicken Poochikian, Joseph Ganz, Dr. John and Elizabeth Zinner, Dr. Hirsch Handmaker, Marc Furstenberg, and Dr. Steve Weissman. I'm also extremely grateful to the late Dr. Hyatt Williams, who understood the self-deception of delinquents better than anyone I've ever known.

Members of my two study groups—one in New York and the other in DC—put up with my numerous digressions while trying to discuss clinical matters not related to Trump. I thank each of you individually, collectively, and alphabetically—Janet Black, Linda Dickson, Cary Gallaudet, Connie Kagel, Jaedene Levy, Micki Penn, Gloria Oviedo, Fran Rosenfeld, Denise Schauer, Linda Schwartz, and Pat Slatt.

There are some faraway people I know mostly through the Internet but who have helped along the way. Robin Bisio, who kept finding useful articles; Thomas Farrell, who kept me abreast of everything *New York Times*; and my first virtual friend—since before *Bush on the Couch*—Chip Yost. Along the way, I reconnected with my long-lost cousin who lives in Montana, Paul Cohn, a writer in his own right and a regular source of ideas and support. Anthony de Mare, dragged into this unwillingly, kept the New York trains running. Allison Thomas sometimes added ideas, and even managed to share a cup of tea with me in LA. And from Santa Monica, newly discovered virtual kindred spirit Jack Neworth sends me his latest thoughts about our current president.

Then there is family: My brilliant sister, Ellen, added clarity and concern about the importance of this book. She was the first to know that Trump was going to become president immediately upon watching him take that escalator to announce his candidacy. My brother-in-law, Steve, was always encouraging, as was my energetic Bushwick niece, Nyssa. Then there is the Perram clan—Tony and Shirley and their lively and loving daughters, Noël, Carolyn, and Elise. Thank you all. Tony, the articles you sent me over this past year—as well as your thoughts—helped me more than you can know. Noël's daughter Beth and her husband, Bryan, even lent me their Rehoboth beach house as a writing retreat. Noel's other daughter, Shannon, is effervescently supportive. For those who don't know, the oldest Perram sister is also my wife, Heather, who I'm always happy to thank again.

I have three different and equally thoughtful, smart, and loving children—Joey, Abe, and Ginevra. You've always been there in so many different ways: Joey, you have been teeming both with great ideas and unexpected sources of information; Abe, you are the writer I'm hoping to become, and I always welcome your positive criticism; and Ginevra, you have been close by in DC most of this time and help, encourage, and remind me why this book is so important for all of us. And there is my daughter-in-law, Emily, whose enthusiasm and thoughtfulness are a wonderful addition to my life—as are her sister, Clare, and their parents, Ann and Sean. Toniann Fernandez keeps my son Joey sane, and keeps me grounded—not only with her love for Bruce Springsteen. My three Portuguese water dogs, Onda, Lilly, and Teddy—for Onda, this is her third book; Lilly's second; Teddy's first. They all need to bark less and lick more. Their dog-friends Ben and Stanley help calm them down.

This has been quite a journey, and I'm taking a deep breath, as President Trump is only a few months into his second year in office. That breath would not have been as smooth or as deep without copy editor extraordinaire Kathleen Go—and never again will I write "towards."

The urgency with which I approached this unique project cannot be overestimated, however. George W. Bush made me uneasy, Barack Obama perplexed and confused me, and Donald Trump just scares me in new and unexpected ways—mostly because of his attacks on American institutions and small-d democracy. But I've tried to do my best to analyze and understand who he is and how he got to be that way—hopefully keeping my political views from interfering too much, which remains a hard-won but necessary struggle. And none of this would have been possible at all without years of knowing and working with many patients who enriched my life, understanding, and appreciation of the human condition.

INDEX